I0102788

ESCAPE TO COLLEGE

Your Guide to Breakin' Out of the 'Hood'

Ida Byrd-Hill

Upheaval Media
Detroit, MI 48224

© 2010 Ida Byrd-Hill
All rights reserved.

No part of this book may be reproduced in any form or by any electronic or mechanical means including information storage and retrieval systems—except in the case of brief quotations embodied in critical articles or reviews, or in the case of the exercises in this book solely for the personal use of the purchaser – without permission in writing from the publisher, Upheaval Media, Inc.

Published by

Upheaval Media, Inc. P.O. Box 241488 Detroit, MI 48224

Book Orders/ Seminars/ Speaking Engagements
call 877-429-2370 FAX 313-221-9494 info@upheavalmedia.net

LIBRARY OF CONGRESS CONTROL NUMBER
2010925246

Byrd-Hill, Ida
Escape to College
ISBN (pbk.) 978-0-615-36266-3
Includes bibliographic references and index

1.   Career Exploration   2. College Preparation   3. Goal Setting
4.   Workforce Development 5. Standardized Exams 6.Urban Life

Printed in the United States of America

Ida Byrd-Hill with her twins, Kevin and Karen Hill
Article, Helping Our Children Achieve Excellence
Photo Courtesy of Essence Magazine

I dedicate this book to God who dropped it into my mind one Sunday to expand the community campaign I had begun in workshop format. I hope it energizes you to move into action as it moved me.

Ida Byrd-Hill

NEED SOME MOTIVATION? GRADE POINT 2.0 TO 3.0.?

Uplift, Inc. is managing an **ESCAPE TO COLLEGE** Scholarship Fund.

Entrance criteria is easy. Guess the name of the college/ university on the front cover.

Go to www.upliftinc.org. Click the **ESCAPE TO COLLEGE** tab.

Deadline June 1, 2010

FORWORD

"Ida Byrd-Hill was worried. Her twins' middle school, set in a crumbling Detroit neighborhood, was being targeted by burglars. Not only had they stolen the computers but the break-ins also made her concerned that the children inside weren't safe. So on a warm September morning she marched up to a group of "thuggish-looking" young men playing basketball behind the school. She walked right onto the court, looked over the rim of her glasses, and told the men she needed to talk to them.

As she recalls the encounter from her suburban Detroit home, her signature burgundy lipstick curls into a smile. Everything about the 43-year-old says she is somebody's mama. She has a no-nonsense lilt to her speech and a paralyzing stare. That was the look she gave the young men the day she told them that they needed to "give a damn" about more than hoops. She asked them to look out for the school kids and to watch over the building, because it was everyone's job to make sure the children got an education.

The men promised--and that was that. "Never had another break in at that school," Byrd-Hill says with a satisfied nod.

For her, the incident is emblematic of the kind of activism needed in her city"

This book is the beginning of an urban workforce revolution. Join the revolution. Register at www.escapetocollege.com. Click on **Join the Revolution** link.

Helping Our Children Achieve Excellence article
Essence Magazine
May 2010

TABLE OF CONTENTS

INTRODUCTION

With both of your parents as high school dropouts, their past certainly impacts one's life and every decision you make. My father, William C. Byrd, was the typical cool kid in high school who never focused on academics as he was a natural entrepreneur. He hated school. My mother, Mary L. Byrd Williams, was the classic brainiac who was forced to dropout of high school as she was pregnant with my brother in the 11th grade in 1965. Back then, pregnant girls did not attend regular high school. My parents wed, but my mother for 17 years hated her life. Her decisions would have been different if she had not dropped out of high school if she had not had 3 babies before age 22. I vowed at 5 years of age I would be the first of their children to graduate from college. The process was not as easy as saying, "I am going to college."

My parents divorced in 1981 and we moved into a roach infested housing project in Flint MI. Did I forget to mention, my father owned a trucking firm, William C. Byrd Trucking with 5 diesels and 20 dump trucks. For a decade I lived in the suburbs of Mt. Morris Twp. I had never seen 1 roach, let alone thousand of them.

A roach was the least of my concern. Remember, I was a suburban preppy bookworm kid dropped into a housing project. I wore plaid skirts, oxford shirts and penny loafers with no socks, and spoke proper English. I looked different, I spoke different and I thought different. Most girls in the 'hood' dreamed of having a baby and living with a man before age 16. Not me. I was college bound through heaven and hell. Little did I know the amount of hell I would endure within the African American community.

Everyone in my community including church member had something negative to say about me and my voracious appetite for books. Yes, I always carried a book. I have read 1 book a week for 35 years since 3rd grade. I have even read the Oxford dictionary cover to cover at age 15. Books took mind across the world while my body lived in the 'hood." But everyone thought I was crazy and loudly told me I was. What perplexed me is most people knew nothing about me as I was a true bookworm – shy, quiet and reserved. (*Boy, time changes a lot of things!*) I have been called every moniker in the English language and maybe other languages, too. My mother says I was born a fighter. I was going to keep my vow to graduate from college and become a physician even if it meant fighting the world. I did graduate from high school. I crossed the stage of Flint Northwestern High School 5th in my class with an ACT score in the 80th percentile providing me 11 college acceptances. I chose the University of Michigan - Ann Arbor as they provided a full financial package.

After surviving a low GPA my first college semester, I worked at the University of Michigan Hospital on the oncology floor to discover I could not handle the emotional trauma that sickness brings. I quickly began the search for a practical career as medicine was out the picture. I landed in Economics after taking a class. Most people hate Economics, yet it was a natural fit for me. I have always loved what money can do for me. I was an entrepreneur from age 11 beginning with a newspaper route, baby sitting, and treat store. I graduated in 1989 with a Bachelor's in Economics and moved into the corporate world first in Human Resources and then Financial Planning. I was good at both. There is no other euphoria that matches the feeling of receiving a check for $400,000, $267,000, $100,000 or even $50,000 for selling your services legally. Yet, it was not my passion. I made a lot of money at both and lived an exciting comforting lifestyle. So why was I so unhappy?

Twice in my life I chose a career not based on passion but safety. My parents wanted me to be a physician that was their dream. I chose Economics so I would always find a job in any industry. Unfortunately, life is not about a job. It is about fulfilling a life mission - a life passion. I desired to be a fashion designer, a creative, an idea person. We, the urban community, have embraced the concept of getting a job and not the pursuit of a passion or dream.

Shouldn't your career be a blast of fun rather than a chore, especially since you spend so much time entrenched in it? Shouldn't you wake up every morning raring to go to your workplace? But more importantly, your career is the fuel to your dream.

Everyone has a dream lifestyle they desire to live. Unfortunately, many people never fulfill their dream or lifestyle. Free yourself. Find a career you love. Create the lifestyle you desire.

This book is a college preparation and a career exploration guide to assist you find your passion as that passion is your passport to Escape to College and break out of the 'hood.'

For the purpose of this book, '**hood**' is not a geographic location in the inner city. It is the description of a mental place that prevents you for reaching the greatest heights of society that you can dream of. It limits your ability to dream and implement that dream. Individuals of any ethnic, social or economic group are included in this 'hood.'

CHAPTER 1   JETSON AGE

Remember the cartoon, the Jetsons, the Hanna-Barbera cartoon created in the fifties and sixties, to depict the future. I fondly remember George, Jane, Judy, Elroy, Rosie the robot servant, Mr. Spacely, Flying cars, Video Phones, moving sidewalks shuttling people from place to place.

While The Jetsons cartoon was fantasy in 1950, sixty years later, it has become a reality today in 2010. The Jetsons cartoon was prophetic as many of the inventions within the cartoon are coming into existence. Many of these inventions today seem to be a normal part of life although in the 1950's they were farfetched. The have evolved straight out of science fiction. It is amazing the change that has occurred within the past 59 years. As people crave more technology, innovative world changing products are being created at rapid pace ushering

the Jetson Age into full force in 2009/2010. Here are some of those inventions.

Movator and air tram at Detroit Metropolitan Airport.

Visit any new airport, such as Detroit Metropolitan Airport. People are moved quickly by the movator- a moveable sidewalk or air tram to their gate. These small inventions seem just right for the aching feet.

The Flying Car at Gas Pump

The Terrafugia uses unleaded gasoline like a regular car but it can get you to your destination faster a cruising flight speed of 115 mph (100 km; 185 km/h). It drives on the road On the highway, it can drive up to 65 mph (105 km/h) to keep up with traffic. The Transition prototype's folded dimensions of 6 ft 9 in (2.1 m) high, 6 ft 8 in (2.0 m) wide and 18 ft 9 in (5.7 m) long are designed to fit within a standard household garage. When operated as a car, the engine powers the front wheel drive. In flight, the engine drives a pusher propeller.[1]

The Transition's layout with folding wings, pusher propeller and twin tail. See it in its first flight March 5, 2009 at the Pittsburgh International Airport.[2] The Terrafugia Transition® flying in formation with the chase aircraft.

Bigelow Aerospace Space Hotel Genesis [3]

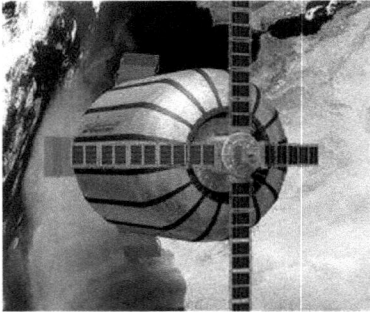

Genesis II, the second prototype expandable space habitat launched by Bigelow Aerospace on June 28, 2007, has completed its 10,000th orbit around the Earth. Following the first spacecraft Genesis I, this unmanned vehicle demonstrates the continued development of future space stations technologies.

Orbiting 665 days and having traveled close to 270 million miles, Genesis II has been busy transmitting pressure, temperature and radiation data to the mission operations staff in Las Vegas.[4] People could be living in space by 2011 on one of these space habitats. It seems like that would be possible fifty years from today but that is 2 ½ years away. Everything you would find in land based hotel you would find in a space hotel except noisy neighbors as the space hotel is millions of miles from its closest neighbor, we think!

White Knight Two[5]

White Knight Two is a jet-powered carrier aircraft which will be used to launch the SpaceShip Two spacecraft. Sir Richard Branson's space tourism company, Virgin Galactic, provided a glimpse today of the completed mother ship that it hopes will ferry adventuresome travelers to the fringes of space.

The White Knight Two (WK2) aircraft--dubbed Eve after Branson's mother--features a twin cockpit construction with a space between the dual cabs for the passenger vehicle, called SpaceShip Two.

The $100 million white craft sports a B29-bomber size wingspan of 140 feet (43 meters), and its four engines are designed to send it soaring as high as 50,000 feet. Once there, its payload, the SpaceShip Two, will detach and climb to over 60 miles (100 kilometers) above Earth The $100 million white craft sports a B29-bomber size wingspan of 140 feet (43 meters), and its four engines are designed to send it soaring as high as 50,000 feet. Once there, its payload, the SpaceShip Two, will detach and climb to over 60 miles (100 kilometers) above Earth treat tourists to several minutes of weightlessness as well as what Virgin Galactic says ought to be a spectacular view. About 250 thrill seekers (including wheelchair-bound physicist Stephen Hawking) have already ponied up $200,000 to reserve a seat on the spacecraft. An official launch date has not been announced, but the company says it hopes to have WK2 aloft with its first complement of newfound astronauts perhaps as early as next year.

Robot Extracts Wounded Soldiers

Being developed by Vecna Technologies, the BEAR - The Battlefield Extraction-Assist Robot - primarily works to remove wounded soldiers from active fire zones safely while withstanding bullets and gunfire. BEAR is capable of lifting heavy loads -- 400 to 500 pounds -- and remaining balanced while navigating rough terrain and even stairs.

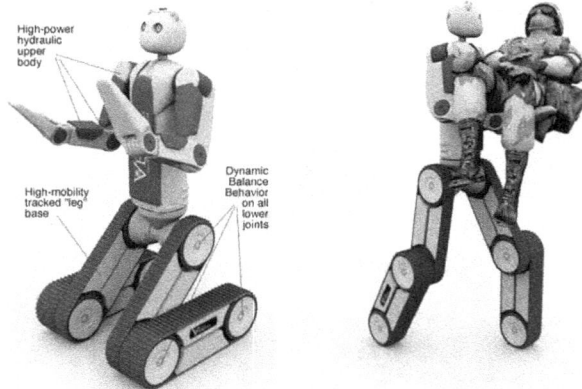

High-power hydraulic upper body

High-mobility tracked "leg" base

Dynamic Balance Behavior on all lower joints

The BEAR's legs allow it to walk upright like a person or they can be folded under the robot and used like tank treads.[6] Imagine this robot scooping up a wounded soldier. Or better yet, a police force made up of these robot soldiers. The Jetson age is here already!

Jupiter, the robot servant
Created in South Korea, the bots, according to the Ministry, will be able to perform such household tasks as cleaning, monitoring homes, reading to children, and ordering pizza via the Internet. [7]

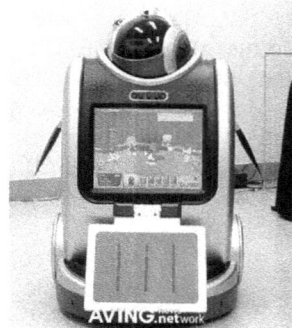

iPhone/ Smart phone touch screen cell phone

An internet-connected multimedia smart phone designed and marketed by Apple Inc. It launched January 2007. Its minimal hardware interface lacks a physical keyboard, so a virtual keyboard is rendered on a multi-touch screen. The iPhone functions as a camera phone, text messenger with visual voicemail. It has a portable media player like the iPod. It also has internet application of email, web browsing and wi-fi connectivity, meaning you can go into any McDonalds or Starbucks and connect to their wi-fi. On January 21, 2009, Apple announced sales of 4.36 million iPhone 3Gs in the first quarter of fiscal 2009, ending December 2008, totaling 17.4 million iPhones to date. Sales in Q4 2008 surpassed temporarily those of Blackberry sales of 5.2 million units, which made Apple briefly the third largest mobile phone manufacturer by revenue, after Nokia and Samsung. [8]

The camera in these phones have the capacity for video telephony where people can talk on the phone while watching the listener. It is coming soon.

Video Games Consoles/ software

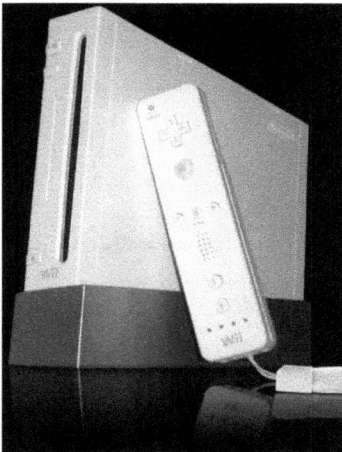

Video gaming is gaining momentum even in a shaky economy. Nintendo says it has sold more than 10 million units of the Wii Play in the United States since its release about two years ago, making the collection of video games among the best-selling games ever. [9] It has sold 49 million game console since its inception surpassing X-box360 who sold 30 million and Playstation 3 who sold 21.6 million. Overall video game unit sales across the world's three largest markets rose by 11% in 2008. In the United States, 268.4 million video game software units were sold last year, an increase of 36 million over 2007.

Video gaming is no longer child's play. Average video gamer is 35 years of age with 49% of the population between 18-49.Video gaming challenges a person's brain especially since participants spend hours of time playing the game. It appears many people believe this fact as sixty-five percent of American households play computer or video games. Women age 18 or older represent a significantly greater portion of the game-playing population (33%) than boys age 17 or younger (18%). Eighty-five percent of all games sold in 2007 were rated "E" for Everyone,

"T" for Teen, or "E10+" for Everyone 10+. Ninety-four percent of game players under the age of 18 report that their parents are present when they purchase or rent games. Sixty-three percent of parents believe games are a positive part of their children's lives. The average adult gamer has been playing video games for 13 years. [10]

Demographic Profile of US Adults Who Play Video Games*, October-December 2007 (% of respondents in each group)

Gender	
Male	55%
Female	50%
Age	
18-29	81%
30-49	60%
50-64	40%
65+	23%
Household income	
<$30,000	52%
$30,000-$49,999	59%
$50,000-$74,999	62%
$75,000+	56%
Education	
Less than high school	40%
High school graduate	51%
Some college/college graduate	57%
Ethnicity/race	
White, non-Hispanic	51%
Black, non-Hispanic	51%
Hispanic (English-speaking)	63%
Community type	
Urban	56%
Suburban	53%
Rural	47%
All adults	**53%**

Note: n=2,054; *play games online or offline using a computer, mobile phone or any other gaming device
Source: Pew Internet & American Life Project, "Adults and Video Games," December 7, 2008

Netbooks are small portable laptop computer designed for wireless communication and access to the Internet primarily designed for web browsing and emailing. Netbooks rely heavily on the Internet for remote access to web-based applications " and are targeted increasingly at users who require a less powerful computer.

" Asustek—Quanta's archrival in Taiwan and the world's seventh-largest notebook maker—began crafting its own inexpensive, low-performance computer. It, too, would be built cheaply using Linux, flash memory, and a tiny 7-inch screen. It had no DVD drive and wasn't potent enough to run programs like Photoshop. Indeed, Asustek intended it mainly just for checking email and surfing the Web. Their customers, they figured, would be children, seniors, and the emerging middle class in India or China who can't afford a full $1,000 laptop. What happened was something entirely different. When Asustek launched the Eee PC in fall 2007, it sold out the entire 350,000-unit inventory in a few months. Eee PCs weren't bought by people in poor countries but by middle-class consumers in western Europe and the US, people who wanted a second laptop to carry in a handbag for peeking at YouTube or Facebook wherever they were. By the end of 2008, Asustek had sold 5 million netbooks, and other brands together had sold 10 million.

Clive Thompson in the article, "The Netbook Effect: How Cheap Little Laptops Hit the Big Time, WIRED magazine 2/23/2009" states, "It turns out that about 95 percent of what I do on a computer can now be accomplished through a browser. I use it for updating Twitter and Facebook and for blogging. Meebo.com lets me log into several instant-messaging accounts simultaneously. Last.fm gives me tunes, and webmail does the email. I use Google Docs for word processing, and if I need to record video, I can do it directly from webcam to YouTube. Come to think of it, because none of my documents reside on the netbook, I'm not sure I even need the trash can." [11]

But the greatest world changing invention of them all is web conferencing.

Web Conferencing
People once traveled to meetings, conferences and seminars. Now individuals can group from all over the world without leaving their desk. Web conferencing is used to conduct live meetings, training, or presentations via the Internet. In a web conference, each participant sits at his or her own computer and is connected to other participants via the internet. Participants can listen to a speaker and view his/her
- Slide show presentations
- Live or Streaming video - where full motion webcam, digital video camera or multi-media files are pushed to the audience.
- Web tours
- Whiteboard - the modern day chalkboard
- Polls and surveys (allows the presenter to conduct questions with multiple choice answers directed to the audience)

And even

- Share screens, desktop or applications

Particpants can have discussions with other particpants and the speaker either via voice or chat. The entire meeting is recorded for later viewing

This technology once extremely expensive and utilized by the large businesses or universities is now provided free through open source software. Anybody with a computer and microphone/telephone can provide training across the globe.

Do you own any of these inventions, like the iPhone/ smart phone or netbook? If not, get ready! These inventions are changing they way we interact and hence they are changing the world.

"Human creativity is the ultimate economic resource. The ability to come up with new ideas and better ways of doing things is ultimately what raises productivity and thus living standards. The great transition from the agricultural age to the industrial age was... based upon natural resources and physical labor power... ultimately giving rise to giant factory complexes in places like Detroit. The previous shift substituted one set of physical inputs (land and human labor) for another (raw materials and physical labor) while the current one is based fundamentally on human intelligence, knowledge and creativity." [12]

Hard labor, once done in factories, has come to an end. The smart, intelligent, creative, technological people will RULE the world and its jobs. Will you be one of them? Or will you complain that there are no jobs and let the world past you by?

The creative class includes scientists, engineers, musicians, designers and knowledge-based professionals who often are based in some high-tech creative industry. In 1900 fewer than 10 percent of Americans were doing creative work. In 1980, the figure was less than 20 percent. By 2000 the figure reached 25 to 30 percent accounting for $1.7 trillion dollars in wage and salary income in America, which is half of all wage and salary surpassing manufacturing and service industries combined. The creative class and jobs within that industry will continually grow as indicated by the graph above. [13] These industries are creating products to move us further into the space age popularized by the cartoon, The Jetsons.

FASTEST GROWING OCCUPATION
through 2016

Source: Bureau of Labor Statistics

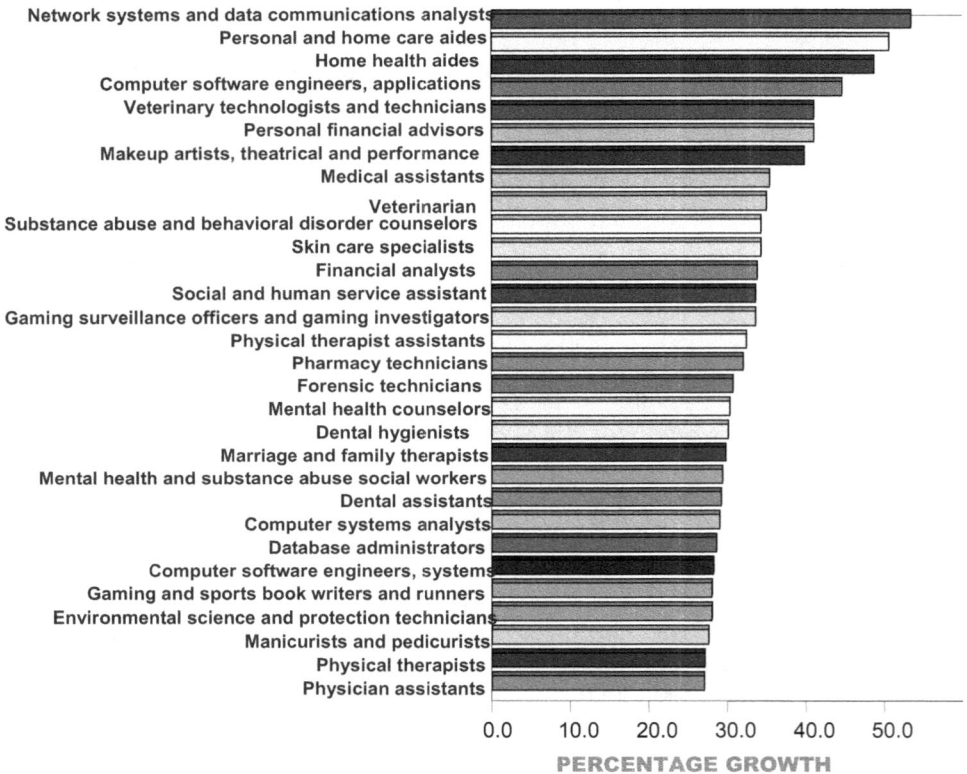

Occupation	Percentage Growth
Network systems and data communications analysts	
Personal and home care aides	
Home health aides	
Computer software engineers, applications	
Veterinary technologists and technicians	
Personal financial advisors	
Makeup artists, theatrical and performance	
Medical assistants	
Veterinarian	
Substance abuse and behavioral disorder counselors	
Skin care specialists	
Financial analysts	
Social and human service assistant	
Gaming surveillance officers and gaming investigators	
Physical therapist assistants	
Pharmacy technicians	
Forensic technicians	
Mental health counselors	
Dental hygienists	
Marriage and family therapists	
Mental health and substance abuse social workers	
Dental assistants	
Computer systems analysts	
Database administrators	
Computer software engineers, systems	
Gaming and sports book writers and runners	
Environmental science and protection technicians	
Manicurists and pedicurists	
Physical therapists	
Physician assistants	

0.0   10.0   20.0   30.0   40.0   50.0

PERCENTAGE GROWTH

Are you preparing for one of these high-demand, high-paying jobs? Your foreign student colleagues are.

When this creative revolution began, America was the dominant player. Many of these creative industry companies had their roots in Silicon Valley – San Francisco Bay, home of Stanford University and University of California- Berkley. As the competition has grown, the dominant players have shifted overseas. In fact, four of the ten products shown above were created in other countries: Jupiter – South Korea, White Knight Two – Britain, Wii console –Japan, Netbooks - Taiwan. It appears foreign corporations are becoming dominant creative players throughout the world when they were once cheap manufacturers. Even in simple technology like the cell phone, America only has one leader – Motorola. The other leaders are based in Finland, South Korea and Japan. America has produced and sold 14.3% of the world's market share of cell phones down 7% from the market share a year ago. Even in the recession people are buying phones they just are not buying American.[14]

Company	2007Sales	2007 Market Share (%)	2006Sales	2006 Market Share (%)
Nokia	435,453.1	37.8	344,915.9	34.8
Motorola	164,307.0	14.3	209,250.9	21.1
Samsung	154,540.7	13.4	116,480.1	11.8
Sony Ericsson	101,358.4	8.8	73,641.6	7.4
LG	78,576.3	6.8	61,986.0	6.3
Others	218,604.3	18.9	184,588.0	18.6
TOTAL	1,152,839.8	100.0	990,862.5	100.0

Note* This table includes iDEN shipments, but excludes ODM to OEM shipments.
Source: Gartner (February 2008)

The irony of this shift in dominant creative corporate players is anchored in education. American dominance the past 20 years was fueled by foreign students. A landmark study by UC Berkeley city planner, Prof. Anna Lee Saxenian, found that, in 1998, Chinese and Indian computer scientists and engineers operated 25 percent of high-tech firms in the San Francisco Bay region - and accounted for more than 58,000 jobs and almost $17 billion in sales.

JOBS! JOBS! JOBS! Don't you aspire to have a high paying job. Basic economics is to supply what is demanded. This race to prepare students for occupations in the Science, Technology

Engineering and Mathematics (STEM) industries is fueled by economic necessity. Corporations are moving their facilities to places where there is a skilled workforce they desire bringing jobs, business opportunities and increased standard of living. In the past only the industrialized countries of Western Europe could compete for these factories, plants and facilities, however the countries where their students possess 21st century skills can compete and beat out industrialized nations.

The Partnership for 21st Century Skills has defined skills that are most crucial for students' success in the competitive global economy.[15] Those skills are:

Thinking critically and making judgments about the barrage of information that comes their way every day—on the Web, in the media, in homes, workplaces and everywhere else. Critical thinking empowers Americans to assess the credibility, accuracy and value of information, analyze and evaluate information, make reasoned decisions and take purposeful action.

Solving complex, multidisciplinary, open-ended problems that all workers, in every kind of workplace, encounter routinely. Businesses expect employees at all levels to identify problems, think through solutions and alternatives, and explore new options if their approaches don't pan out.

Creativity and entrepreneurial thinking—a skill set highly associated with job creation. Many of the fastest-growing jobs and emerging industries rely on workers' creative capacity—the ability to think unconventionally, question the herd, imagine new scenarios and produce astonishing work. Likewise, Americans can create jobs for themselves and others with an entrepreneurial mindset—the ability to recognize and act on opportunities and the willingness to embrace risk and responsibility, for example.

Communicating and collaborating with teams of people across cultural, geographic and language boundaries — a necessity in diverse and multinational workplaces and communities.

Innovative use of knowledge, information and opportunities to create new services, processes and products. The global marketplace rewards organizations that rapidly and routinely find better ways of doing things. Companies want workers who can contribute in this environment.

Corporations are seeking employees with these skill sets and are moving around the globe to secure those employees. Reeling from the Asian financial crisis of 1997, South Korea decided that becoming a high-tech nation was the only way to secure its future.[16] The government offered information technology courses to homemakers, subsidized computers for low-income families and made the country the first in the world to have high-speed Internet in every primary, junior and high school.

South Korea was not the only Asian country to make that decision and retool first its Universities and then its k-12 educational Systems. China led the decision in 1979 with the creation of China Central Radio and TV University (CCRTVU) a dedicated open and distance education institution, under the direct supervision of the Ministry of Education of P.R. China which offers, on a nationwide basis, multi-media courses through radio, TV, print, audio-visual materials and computer networks.[17]

At present, CCRTVU is responsible for educating 2.6 million students annually via radio, TV, print, audio-visual materials and computer networks. China Central Radio and TV University (CCRTVU) consist of 44 provincial Radio and TV Universities (PRTVUs), 841 branch schools at prefecture and city level, and 1,768 work stations. These facilities are important as only 10% of the Chinese population have access to internet. China believes by educating the poor rural students it can lift its standard of living.

In the first 20 years, the China Central Radio and TV University (CCRTVU) has produced over 2.6 million college graduates, 1 million secondary vocational school graduates, 35 million non-degree continuing education and in-service training. The China TV Teachers College (CTVTC) has graduated 710,000 teachers of primary schools and 550,000 teachers of secondary schools and has trained 2 million teachers and 1 million principals of primary and secondary schools. These tech savvy educators are driving the Chinese k-12 educational system in the same manner they were educated via radio, TV, print, audio-visual materials and computer networks.

Malaysia following in the footsteps of its more developed Asian counterparts developed and piloted 88 Smart Schools in 1999 to sustain, "productivity-driven growth, which will be achievable only with a technologically literate, critically thinking work force prepared to participate fully in the global economy of the 21st century. Transforming the educational system will entail…moving away from memory-based learning designed for the average student to an education that stimulates thinking, creativity, and caring in all students, caters to individual abilities and learning styles." [18]This Smart School pilot, where 85,000 students are participating, utilizes the computer and internet to guide student learning. Malaysia is preparing to transform its entire 10,000 schools, 5.8 million students and 450,000 teachers into Smart Schools by 2010.

The United States once ranked as the number one educational system in the world. It has been replaced by Finland, South Korea, Hong-Kong-China.[19] Most people anticipated the Asian countries would dominate in the Math and Science arena except they are dominating in the Reading area as well.[20] These dominate players attribute their educational success to the conversion from highly structured, disciplined, purely memory, teacher –centric classrooms to a more hands-on, independent, student-centric classroom monitored by a sophisticated computer learning management system except for Finland who leaves technology absorption to vocational classes after high school graduation.

Finland's students placed first in science and near the top in math and reading, according to results released late last year. An unofficial tally of Finland's combined scores puts it in first place overall, says Andreas Schleicher, who directs the OECD's test, known as the Programme for International Student

Assessment, or PISA. The U.S. placed in the middle of the pack in math and science; its reading scores were tossed because of a glitch. [21]

According to the article, "What Makes Finnish Kids So Smart?" teachers say extra playtime is one reason for the students' success and another is self-reliant children. Early on, kids do a lot without adults hovering. Once school starts, the Finns are more self-reliant. There is no Internet filter in the school library. They can walk in their socks during class, but at home even the very young are expected to lace up their own skates or put on their own skis. [22]

It appears the theme for the new educational revolution are individualized learning, classes via the computer and internet and more freedom. Students are treated as future leaders equipped with the best to succeed even in countries with high poverty. Hannele Frantsi, a school principal sums it perfectly, "We don't have oil or other riches. Knowledge is the thing Finnish people have,"[23] Research into cognitive development is confirming Dr. Maria Montessori's ideology [24] that the children have an absorbent mind and through the exploration of life, "children develop an insatiable hunger for the acquisition of a particular knowledge or skill." Children given the freedom that is the liberty of the human being, and this freedom allows children to grow in social grace, inner discipline, concentration and joy understanding freedom must be coupled with a prepared environment. [25]

Large corporations are moving away from American inner cities to developing nations to acquire the desired workforce skills especially since corporate leaders *perceive* those skills are in short supply in American inner cities. American cities are drowning under the weight of negativity caused by high school dropouts, when they should be growing, hustling and bustling places full of vibrant energy and prosperous economies.

But this can change, if you the student decide you want to participate in the global competition by a high-demand high-paying career that often requires a college degree.

CHAPTER 2   EDUCATION PAYS!!!

A person with a college degree earns more than a person without a high school diploma. **"Whoever said education does not pay,"** have never looked at the following picture.

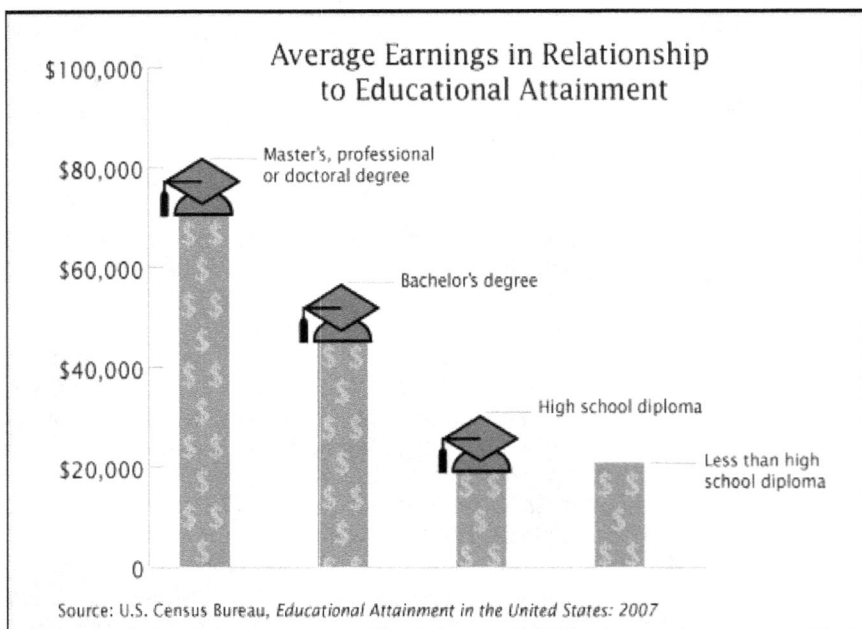

Average Earnings in Relationship to Educational Attainment

Source: U.S. Census Bureau, *Educational Attainment in the United States: 2007*

More education continues to pay off in a big way

- Adults with advanced degrees earn four times more than those with less than a high school diploma. Workers 18 and older with a master's, professional or doctoral degree earned an average of $82,320 in 2006, while those with less than a high school diploma earned $20,873.

- Workers 18 and older with a bachelor's degree earned an average of $56,788 in 2006, while those with a high school diploma earned $31,071.

- Among those whose highest level of education was a high school diploma or equivalent, non-Hispanic white workers had the highest average earnings ($32,931), followed by Asians ($29,426) and blacks ($26,268). Average earnings of Hispanic workers in the same group ($27,508) were not statistically different from those of Asian or black workers.

- Among workers with advanced degrees, Asians ($88,408) and non-Hispanic whites ($83,785) had higher average earnings than Hispanics ($70,432) and blacks ($64,834).

Who Goes to College and earns an Advanced Degree?

Women and Asians

- **One-third of young women have bachelor's degrees** (about 33 percent of young women 25 to 29 had a bachelor's degree or more education in 2007, compared with 26 percent of their male counterparts)

- In 2007, 86 percent of all adults 25 and older reported they had completed at least high school and 29 percent at least a bachelor's degree.

- More than half of Asians 25 and older had a bachelor's degree or more (52 percent), compared with 32 percent of non-Hispanic whites, 19 percent of blacks and 13 percent of Hispanics

- Among workers with advanced degrees, Asians ($88,408) and non-Hispanic whites ($83,785) had higher average earnings than Hispanics ($70,432) and blacks ($64,834).

In many urban communities, like Detroit, being smart is synonymous with being the unpopular brainiac girl or boy nerd.

We all want to be cool and popular, I know I did. Unfortunately, the cool guy in middle school and high school is no longer cool after high school. The cool people after college are the brainiacs and nerds. Ever heard of the movie, Revenge of the Nerds? The world after high school is certainly the revenge of the nerds. The world is run by brainiac girls and nerdy boys as they have the money, power, fast cars, beautiful mates, mansions, jobs, and positions. Look at the earnings chart. The person without a high school diploma over 40 years earned 1 million dollars compared to the person with a professional degree who earned 4.4 million over the same 40 years. That is a 3.4 million dollar difference.

Over a Lifetime the Earnings Gap is Staggering

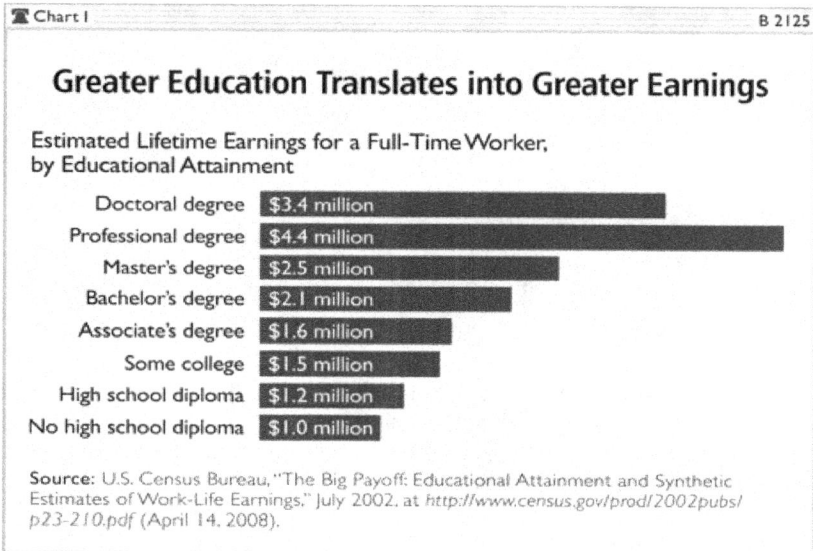

Chart I   B 2125

Greater Education Translates into Greater Earnings

Estimated Lifetime Earnings for a Full-Time Worker,
by Educational Attainment

Doctoral degree	$3.4 million
Professional degree	$4.4 million
Master's degree	$2.5 million
Bachelor's degree	$2.1 million
Associate's degree	$1.6 million
Some college	$1.5 million
High school diploma	$1.2 million
No high school diploma	$1.0 million

Source: U.S. Census Bureau, "The Big Payoff: Educational Attainment and Synthetic Estimates of Work-Life Earnings," July 2002, at *http://www.census.gov/prod/2002pubs/p23-210.pdf* (April 14, 2008).

They have all the fun as they the money to have fun. They look like they are being tortured in high school, but in the end they become the cool people. President Barack Obama and First Lady Michelle are a fine example. They are the classic Nerd and Brainiac. They both have Juris Doctors (J.D.) (law degrees). President Obama has a J.D. from Harvard Law University after receiving an undergraduate degree from Columbia University. Michelle Obama also has a J.D. from Harvard Law University after receiving an undergraduate degree from Princeton University. To graduate from both universities, it requires superior study skills, a high school grade point average of 3.5 or higher. This is the true sign of a nerd or brainiac.

Do you think it is cool to be trotted around the world in Air Force One – the presidential airplane?

If you desire an affluent lifestyle, you certainly must get postsecondary training—college, or skilled trades apprenticeship. Let that statement sink into your spirit. **"You must get postsecondary training."**

Be the contrarian you really are and buck the trend that occurs in your neighborhood.

BE smart ---
GET a high grade point average---
GRADUATE from high school ---
GO to college or skilled trades apprenticeship.
FINISH.

Make a commitment you will achieve your dream filled with the houses, cars, clothes, trips, people and the environment you choose as you will complete college with at least an Associate's Degree. In order to be admitted to college, you must graduate high school with the necessary requirements – high grade point average, high college admissions test scores and required classes. Maximize your high school years wisely!!!!

This book is not about being realistic about life, it is about being the real you--- the fun, hilarious, impractical, wild and crazy you that only you know exist.   Complete every assignment as they can lead you to your dream career. You can and should write in this book.

CHAPTER 3   LET HISTORY REPEAT ITSELF

Today, it is a struggle to graduate from an urban high school, let alone graduate from college. Many of us believe education is '**acting white**.' Adolescents are ridiculed by their friends and well-meaning adults for speaking proper English, for striving for academic excellence and for even attempting to graduate from high school.

What is so perplexing is that story of anti-intellectualism, hatred of school or education, is only present in our history since American slavery or indentured servitude. Many of us have descended from these ancient civilizations - Egypt, Carthage, Kush, Aztec, Mayan, China, and Persia - who embraced and birthed academic subjects we still use today.

History always repeats itself in one form or another. The question is, *"Which history to repeat?"* Will it be the ancient history filled with glory, power, wealth and expansion; or modern day history of abuse, slavery, pain and struggle? You choose which history you want to repeat. Don't let people feed you stereotypes and myths based on their version of modern day history. Don't believe them!!! Know the history that transpired prior to our arrival in America. Many of us have descended from powerful, intellectual societies, leaving an ancestral memory of innovation instilled within our genetics. All we have to do is to tap our ancestral history of architectural, scientific, technological and mathematical wonders and allow it to pave a path for your Escape to College.

Civilization memory begins with knowing one's history. While this book provides some highlights of ancient civilizations, it is not intended to be an all-inclusive guide. It is intended to inspire you to perform your own research into your ancestral history to find your genetic memory and present day place in today's society. What is certain, intellectualism will be woven throughout your ancient history and its civilization. Go to www.EscapetoCollege.com and view a few clips of your ancient history. The advancements your civilization created will blow your mind, but will further the expectation you can let history repeat itself within you.

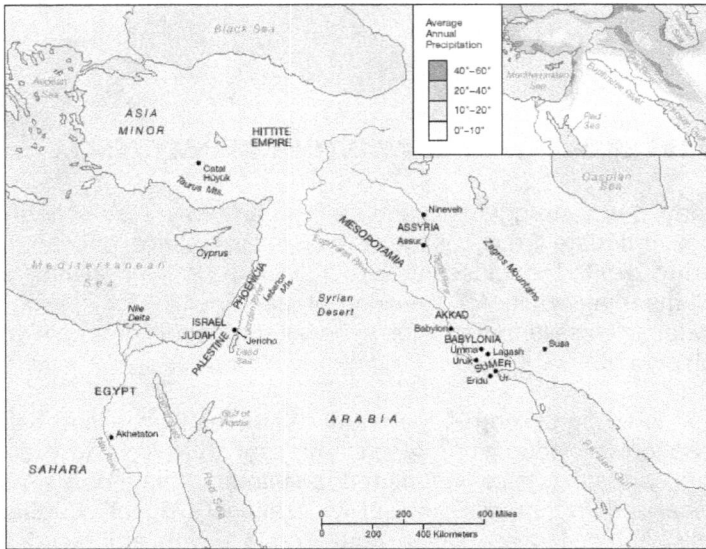

Egypt was an ancient civilization of eastern North Africa, concentrated along the lower reaches of the Nile River in what is now the modern country of Egypt.

The success of ancient Egyptian civilization stemmed partly from its ability to adapt to the conditions of the Nile River Valley. The predictable flooding and controlled irrigation of the fertile valley produced surplus crops, which fueled social development and culture. With resources to spare, the administration sponsored mineral exploitation of the valley and surrounding desert regions, the early development of an independent writing system, the organization of collective construction and agricultural projects, trade with surrounding regions, and a military intended to defeat foreign enemies and assert Egyptian dominance. Motivating and organizing these activities was a bureaucracy of elite scribes, religious leaders, and administrators under the control of a pharaoh who ensured the cooperation and unity of the Egyptian people in the context of an elaborate system of religious beliefs.

Ancient Egyptians were masters in the quarrying, surveying and construction techniques that facilitated the building of monumental pyramids, temples, and obelisks that are still standing. This construction and architectural genius was facilitated by a system of mathematics, including the decimal system, a system of science and technology. Egyptians were the creators of the scientific method a practical and effective system of medicine, irrigation systems and agricultural production techniques, the first known ships, glass technology. They also created their own alphabet and new forms of literature. Egypt left a lasting African legacy of scientific, mathematical and technological inventions. If you are African American there is a possibility you are a descendent of these Africans – Egyptians. Or maybe you descended from Kush/ Cush, or Carthage.

Kush/Cush was an ancient African state centered what is now the Republic of Sudan and Ethopia. It was one of the earliest civilizations to develop in the Nile River Valley. Having also been referred to as Nubia, Kush was the land of gold with gold processing artifacts found in recent years.

Carthage was located above modern day Libya in North Africa shown in red.

THE CARTHAGINIAN EMPIRE 3RD CENTURY BC

While many people assume democracy was created by the Greeks and Romans, that is not entirely the case. Even Aristotle commented favorably on the constitutional government of Carthage, which answered directly to its people. Carthage was best known by Hannibal.He led an almost successful invasion of the then very powerful Rome, attacking them in Spain and Northern Italy, but eventually failed. Hannibal is often connected with elephants because he used elephants against Roman Troops. Little known fact was that Carthag created the most advanced warships in the world. They were dominant as they could sail the Mediterrean and destroy any other countries ship without notice. They lost their dominance when one ship was grounded in Rome and the Roman copied their ship construction.

The **Aztecs** lived in what is now Mexico. The name Mexico comes from the Aztec word *Mexica*, a name they used to describe themselves. Their capital city, Tenochtitlan, was located where Mexico City is today.

Tenochtitlan was built on an island in the middle of Lake Texcoco. Necessity breeds invention and innovation. The Aztecs didn't have any farmland, so they devised a way to create their own farmland, called chinampas The Aztecs wove giant reed mats and placed them on top of the water. They made a fence around the mat and placed mud, silt, and rotten vegetables on it. Then willow trees were planted on all sides of the chinampa. The willow trees grew very quickly and their roots bound the soil to keep it from washing away. The Aztecs planted corn, tomatoes, potatoes, chili peppers, and squash. The plants' roots would grow to the bottom of the lake so they would have an endless supply of water. The chinampas were manmade islands created by piling up mud and vegetation from the bottom of the lake. The size of the chinampas didn't matter; what mattered was if two canoes could pass between the chinampas. The mud that the Aztecs used to build the chinampas was rich in minerals and ideal for growing crops. Tomatoes, avocados, and chili peppers were unheard of in Europe until Spanish explorers brought some back from Aztec lands.

The Aztecs created the calendar to determine the best time for planting crops. One year had 365 days divided into 18 months. Each month had 20 days, and there were 5 extra days at the end of the year, which were thought to be bad-luck days when disasters were most likely to happen. Our modern calendar is based on this invention.

Mayans were a Mesoamerican civilization. The ancient Mayans lived in what is now known as southern Mexico and northern Central America including Guatemala, Belize, Honduras, Yucatan Peninsula and El Salvador. Their descendants still live there today, and many of them speak the Mayan languages.

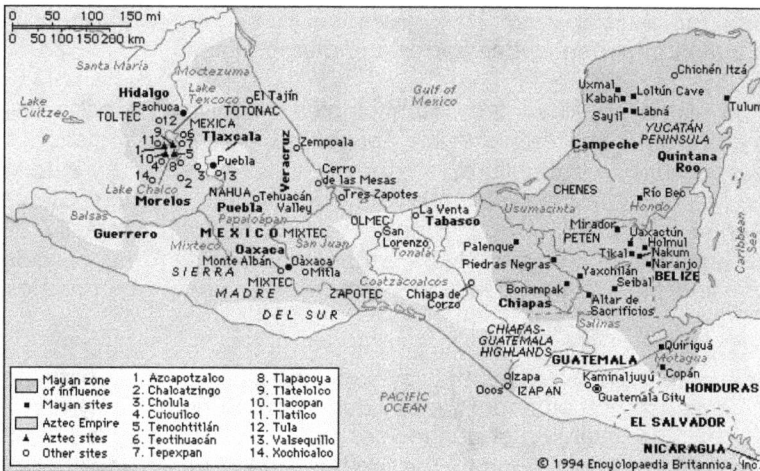

```
0   50  100  150 mi
0  50 100 150 200 km
```

Mayan zone of influence
Mayan sites
Aztec Empire
Aztec sites
Other sites

1. Azcapotzalco
2. Chalcatzingo
3. Cholula
4. Cuicuilco
5. Tenochtitlán
6. Teotihuacán
7. Tepexpan
8. Tlapacoya
9. Tlatelolco
10. Tlacopan
11. Tlatilco
12. Tula
13. Valsequillo
14. Xochicalco

© 1994 Encyclopaedia Britannica, Inc.

They had the most advanced writing system in the Americas prior to European contact. They used sophisticated mathematic systems and had complex and useful cyclical calendars. Spectacular art and monumental architecture were two other notable accomplishments of this civilization.

The Mayans were master architects, building pyramids and even entire cities, many of which are still standing today.

Mayan pyramids were made of stone. The stone was carved to create a stair-step design. On the top of each pyramid was a shrine dedicated to a particular deity. Rituals were thought to influence the Gods were held in these shrines.

The earliest **Chinese** inventions were the abacus, shadow clock, kites and Kongming Lantern. As an astronomically advanced civilization the Ancient Chinese first recorded observations of comets, solar eclipses and supernovae. The 4 greatest inventions of the Ancient Chinese were printing, paper making (the first paper made by pounding linen), gunpowder (made by shamans trying to find a stone of immortality) and the magnetic compass. Ancient Chinese made great advances in metallurgy, For example 2300 years ago no one in Europe or the Middle East could melt one ounce of iron the meanwhile the Chinese were casting multi-ton iron objects. The British were able to replicate this feat in 1200 A.D. The Chinese also learned how to drill for natural gas. They invented row crop farming, silk, porcelain, rudders, wheelbarrows and umbrellas.

The Chinese invented technologies involving mechanics, hydraulics, and mathematics applied to horology, metallurgy, astronomy, agriculture, engineering, music theory, craftsmanship, nautics, and warfare. By the Warring States Period (403–221 BC), they had advanced metallurgic technology, including the blast furnace and cupola furnace, while the finery forge and puddling process were known by the Han Dynasty (202 BC–AD 220).

A sophisticated economic system in China gave birth to inventions such as paper money during the Song Dynasty (960–1279). The invention of gunpowder by the 10th century led to an array of inventions such as the fire lance, land mine, naval mine, hand cannon, exploding cannonballs, multistage rocket, and rocket bombs with aerodynamic wings and explosive payloads. With the navigational aid of the 11th-century compass and ability to steer at high sea with the 1st-century sternpost rudder, premodern Chinese sailors sailed as far as East Africa and Egypt. In water-powered clockworks, the premodern Chinese had used the escapement mechanism since the 8th century and the endless power-transmitting chain drive in the 11th century. They also made large mechanical puppet theaters driven by

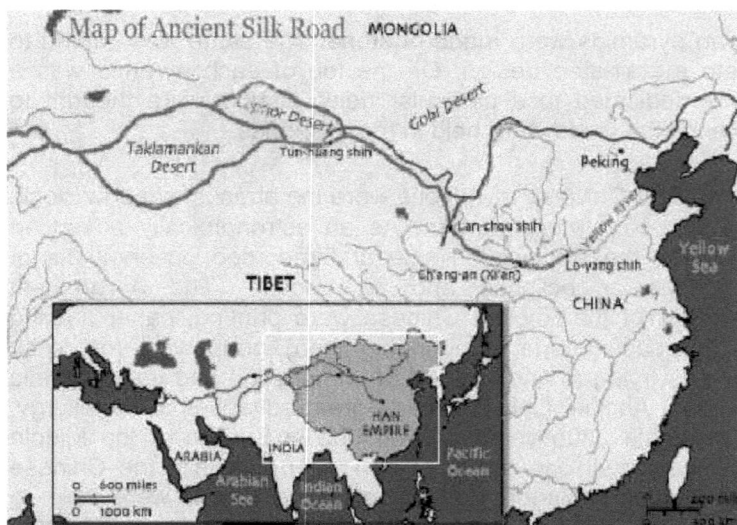

Map of Ancient Silk Road

waterwheels and carriage wheels and wine-serving automatons driven by paddle wheel boats.

The **Persian** Empire started in the north west corner of what is now Iran. It grew through military conquest to cover a huge region that roughly encompasses today's Iran, Iraq, Armenia, Afghanistan, Turkey, Bulgaria, many parts of Greece, Egypt, Syria, much of what is now Pakistan, Jordan, Israel, the West Bank, the Gaza Strip, Lebanon, Caucasia, Central Asia, Libya, and northern parts of Arabia. The empire eventually became the largest empire of the ancient world. Persepolis was the ceremonial capitol of Persia. Susa and Pasargadas also acted as capital cities at different times in Persian history. They were all in what is now Iran.

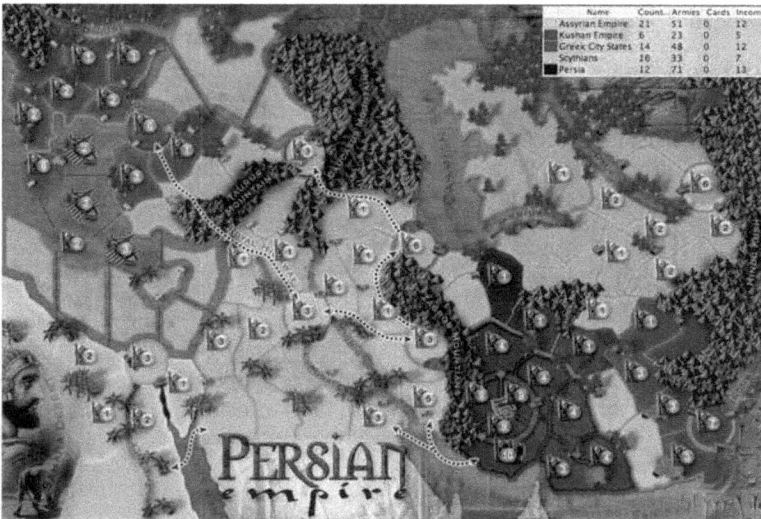

Iran is the oldest continuous civilizations. Today, Iran ranks second in the world in natural gas reserves and also second in oil reserves.It is OPEC's 2nd largest oil exporter. Iran has leading manufacture industry in the fields of car-manufacture and transportation, construction materials, home appliances, food and agricultural goods, armaments, pharmaceuticals, information technology, power and petrochemicals in the Middle East. Iran has the potential to become a energy superpower.

Carpet-weaving is one of the most distinguished manifestations of Persian culture and art, and dates back to ancient Persia. Persians were among the first to use mathematics, geometry and astronomy architecture and also have extraordinary skills in making massive domes which can be seen frequently in the structure of bazaars and mosques. The main building types of classical Iranian architecture are the mosque and the palace. Iran, besides being home to a large number of art houses and galleries, also holds one of the largest jewelry collections in the world.

The first windmill appeared in Iran in the 9th century.-Iranians contributed significantly to the current understanding of astronomy, mathematics, medicine and philosophy. Iranians are still entrenched in medicine with specialties in biotechnology and pharmacology. Most people know of Iran because of it nuclear program.

Iran is the 7th country in production of uranium hexaflouride. Iran now controls the entire cycle for producing nuclear fuel. Iran's current facilities includes several research reactors, an uranium mine, an almost complete commercial nuclear reactor, and uranium processing facilities that include a uranium enrichment plant.

So as you see your ancestors were inventors, creators, educated intellectuals. If you need to physically see your ancestral civilization, go to www.escapetocollege.com and view clips of your specific civilization. Repeat your ancestor's history! Grasp and embrace education, innovation and creativity. Allow others to groom you for greatness today.

CHAPTER 4   AS A MAN THINKETH, SO IS HE.

"*As a man thinketh, so is he.*"[26] This is the famous book written by Paul Allen. Thoughts and ideas are living things. Whatever you think upon is attracted to you. You think upon riches, riches come to you. You think upon poverty, poverty remains with you. You relish the thought of failure, despite your best efforts failure will reside with you. But let you, an ordinary person; believe in success and success finds its way to you. For everything you ask for you receive—whatever you seek you shall find, every door you knock upon will be opened.[27] But the key is in your brain.

Man only uses a small capacity of his brain, which is the greatest computer drawing board in the world. Your mind produces living thoughts and ideas. The more you focus upon thoughts, the more the creative juices in your mind will flow the more visions you will see. Visions are - foresight - the ability to see into the future and devise wise plans. Visions lay out the road map to your dream.

What is Your Dream Odyssey?

The definition of an odyssey is *a long series of wanderings or adventures, especially when filled with notable experiences, hardships. Or an epic voyage* [28] Everyone's life is an odyssey – a book ready to be written- if they chronicled it. Unfortunately many people do not look at their life as an adventure. All they experience is hardship, pain and agony. There is little exciting, daring opportunity, no spunk. People settle for working a dead end job they hate. They settle for bad things. Bad things are guaranteed to happen. It is called Murphy's Law. However we can plan the good experiences – the final destination of our lives. The good and bad experiences make up our epic voyage like Homer's *The Odyssey* where Greek hero Odysseus (or Ulysses, as he was known in Roman myths) and his long journey home following the fall of Troy. It takes Odysseus ten years to reach Ithaca after the ten-year Trojan War.

Your life experience takes time. It will not happen overnight. Spend every day working towards your dream or dream odyssey. What is your dream or dream odyssey?

Let the outrageous crazy adventures be ever present in your memory. These experiences bring joy, triumph and a pride of accomplishment. Don't let the negativity of current life zap your dreams from you.

Yours are the fuel to the creation of your life. It does not matter where you began in the 'hood' in the mansion, you have the power to determine your end and some of the process to get there. Will your end be full of drama, sadness, pain, poverty and anguish? Or will it be full of excitement, happiness, wealth and joy? You have the power to decide. It all begins with your dream and the dream odyssey you create in your mind.

Don't believe me! Imagine if you found a genie bottle and could wish your greatest dreams come true. Your life would be a blast of fun. What experiences would you wish for?

Genie Wish #1

_____

_____

Genie Wish #2

_____

_____

Genie Wish #3

_____

_____

Did you utilize your genie wishes so as to extend your fun for the rest of your life? If no, think about experience that could last a lifetime. Draw pictures of the 3 craziest, outrageous experiences you want to achieve in life. Maybe it is to produce a movie, a CD, own a billion dollar business, build a hotel. Whatever your experience is, draw a picture of it. Do not draw a career or a thing. Draw the ultimate experience you want to achieve. If you can not draw, cut out pictures in magazines and paste them here.

Craziest Outrageous Experience #1

Craziest Outrageous Experience #2

Craziest Outrageous Experience #3

Now describe the pictures in writing.

Craziest Outrageous Experience #1

_____

_____

_____

_____

_____

_____

_____

_____

_____

_____

_____

_____

_____

_____

_____

_____

_____

_____

_____

_____

_____

_____

_____

_____

_____

Craziest Outrageous Experience #2

_____

_____

_____

_____

_____

_____

_____

_____

_____

_____

_____

_____

_____

_____

_____

_____

_____

_____

_____

_____

_____

_____

_____

_____

_____

_____

Craziest Outrageous Experience #3

_____

_____

_____

_____

_____

_____

_____

_____

_____

_____

_____

_____

_____

_____

_____

_____

_____

_____

_____

_____

_____

CHAPTER 5   DREAM, IF YOU DARE!

Dream, if you dare! Forget what parents, teachers and other concerned adults told you about dreaming. Dreaming is not a delusionary activity; neither is your head in the clouds nor are you away from reality. The truth reveals that reality starts as a dream. William James coined this truth briefly *"a man may not achieve everything he has dreamed, but he will never achieve anything great without having dreamed it first."* So dream on! Dare to become great. Soar through the future as Orville and Wilber Wright did in the mechanical bird onto the modern airplane. See the future like Henry Ford who revolutionized the production of the Horseless Carriage, brighten the future as Thomas Edison who dreamed of a day that electricity could be harnessed to produce an everlasting candle of light. Dream I say if you dare!!! For those skeptical folks, dreams, as defined by Webster's dictionary, are "a fond hope or aspiration – thought imagining as possible-a fanciful vision of the conscious mind."

Bill Gates was enrolled in pre-law at Harvard University following in his father's footsteps as a lawyer. But his heart was not in his studies. His passion was computers; he just could not get enough of them. Eventually, he and Paul Allen created the first line of programming code, BASIC, for the, Altair 8080, the first micro computer kit. He knew with this first micro computer every home would soon have a PC. Everyone told him he was crazy. When computers were first invented they cost $600,000+ and literally occupied an entire 2000 square foot room. How could every American afford such a luxury? They could not!!! IBM then approached Bill Gates asking him to write the basic code for their new ROM chips and create an operating system for their computers. He agreed but asked to keep the rights of the DOS operating system that he created. He left Harvard and formed the Microsoft Corporation. Today, 78% of American population use a computer for ordinary tasks and most of those computers run on his software. Could you imagine life without a computer? Personal computers *wouldn't be possible without Bill Gate's operating systems that made him the richest man in the world!*

"What you think is real, is your reality", states Robert Kuyosaki in **_Retire Young, Retire Rich_**! This is the most profound statement I have ever heard. Let me restate it, "Your Reality is what You Think Is Real."

This statement means the things; actions and behaviors around you are only as real as you think they are. Your environment manifests your thoughts. My offices and houses have always been impeccably decorated with upholstered furniture and authentic works of art. They look plush because I feel wealthy and desire plush. I could have saved some money and created a cheaper surrounding but I felt wealthy therefore my environment looks wealthy. No matter how much money you have, if you feel poor then your surroundings would look poor.

Make a commitment that your surroundings would reflect the richness inside of you. I know you are thinking, "I'm just a kid! I have no money. I have no say in how my house, neighborhood or city looks like." Well, you have the power to pick up trash when you see it on your block. You can cut your grass and your neighbors' grass. You can water and maintain your grass until it looks like carpet. You can sweep the sidewalk and your porch until it is crystal clean. You can shovel the sidewalk in the winter. I know as I did these things as a teenager living in a housing project in Flint MI. people laughed at me until our building became so clean, it looked extremely out of place in the midst of tall uncut grass and filthy sidewalks. Many people would come sit on my stoop and on our lawn just to talk. Our tenement looked palatial and inviting. To the point, my neighboring residents decided they needed to do something as well and began to cleanup their areas. I am still the same way 25 years later. Let your richness drive your block, neighborhood, and your city.

Wayne Dyer in his book, **_You'll see it when you believe it_** sums it up in this manner. *"Whatever you focus your thoughts on expands!"* If you have a scarcity mentality, it means that we believe in scarcity and that we evaluate our life in terms of its lack. If we dwell on scarcity, we are putting energy into what we do not have and this continues to be our experience of life. When you live and breathe prosperity with a belief that every thing is in huge supply and that we are all entitled to have all that we can start actively treating yourself and others in this fashion.

Prosperity and abundance is not something that you can manufacture but something that you accept or tune into. Unlimited prosperity and abundance is all around you. The issue is, Can You See It? The answer is, Only If You Believe It! Life, your environment, your city can be changed by changing your beliefs. Belief can be summed up by this poem.

If you *think* you are beaten, you are
If you *think* you dare not, you don't
If you like to win, but you *think*, you can't
It is almost certain you won't.

If you *think* you'll lose, you're lost
For out in the world we find
Success begins with a fellow's will
It's all in the *state of mind*.

If you *think* you are outclassed, you are,
You've got to *think* high to rise

You've got to be *sure of yourself* before
You can ever win a prize.

"Life's battles don't always go
To the stronger or faster man,
But soon or late the man who wins
Is the man **WHO THINKS HE CAN!**"

What is your belief?

Do you believe you can achieve these three craziest, outrageous, things you drew pictures and described? Or are you saying to yourself, "*I am poor!*, *"I will never be rich." "I cannot live rich." "I have struggled for 50 generations." "I have always lived in a rented home." "I have always lived in the projects." "I have never had enough to eat." "No one had every graduated from high school in our family." "No one in this family will ever go to college."*

Cut your pictures and descriptions out of this book or make bigger pictures with descriptions. Place those pictures on the refrigerator or your mirror and repeat these affirmations every single day.

- I choose to be wealthy
- Financial independence is mine
- Money is my friend
- I am comfortable having money
- Large amounts of money are coming to me
- Money flows to me easily and naturally
- The more money I have, the more I can live my dream
- My dream is

  _____

  _____

- I will generate _____ income this year.
- Everyday I am moving closer to my dream.
- I am a money magnet
- I will assist people financially as I become wealthy

My belief has always been that I will become wealthy even while sitting in a housing project in Flint, MI. I believed I was wealthy. I would read those Richie Rich comic books and dreamed of being wealthy. Somewhere it soaked in. In high school when everyone worked a minimum wage job at the local fast food restaurant, I worked at the Library as a page. I loved and still love to read. My passion for books allowed me to earn 1 ½ times minimum wage then. My grades were excellent affording a full ride college scholarship to the University of Michigan. While the scholarship paid for tuition, room and board, I was forced to work to achieve my goal of acquiring $10,000 upon graduation from college. Every job I received earned at least 2 times minimum wage. My belief was that I deserved better than average and that is what I got. Rich thoughts drew me to rich experienced jobs. Opportunities after college seemed to abound as I only saw opportunity.

But as easily as opportunities came they went when I married a man who believed in scarcity, no matter what opportunities were available he saw lack, scarcity and poverty. Despite our six-figure family income we struggled for nine years because of the thoughts of scarcity and poverty were dominant.

When I divorced him and negative thoughts left and my opportunities began to rebound. WHY? The universe contains both abundance and scarcity, rich and poor, good and bad!

Your thoughts are living things, which become the basis of your dream odyssey. Today, my dream odyssey is to retire at age 50 in year 2017 to a tropical island in the Caribbean where I can write bestsellers to encourage millions of people worldwide to grow and expand their wealth consciousness. I expect a multimillionaire dollar net worth to live off. For most people my dream seems rushed and absurd, especially since I have become an educational activist in a recessionary economy. Little do they know, I believe the best way to achieve a goal is to help others achieve the same goal. As I encourage young people they have the ability and power to change their world, I change my world. I have remained focused on the path I have chosen for my dream odyssey. This book, **Escape to College**, **Follow Your Inner Compass**, **My Daily Odyssey Journal**, **Breakin' Out of Your Financial Funk!** and soon to be released **Kiss Teen Turmoil Away!** books, are a part of that dream odyssey. I have a dream I will write 10 books by 2013 [29] You have to determine the first major goal in your dream odyssey is to graduate from high school with the credentials to be admitted to college with scholarships.

Constructing the Path of your Escape to College

Are you making steps to achieve your dream reality? Yes or No. If Yes, What are those steps? Detail them here.

_____

_____

_____

_____

_____

_____

_____

If NO, What steps do you need to make? List them here.

_____

_____

_____

_____

_____

_____

_____

These steps are beginning of your plan to achieve your dream. Yes, I said "Plan." It has been documented that three (3%) percent of the Yale University graduating class of 1953 had a written goals. After 20 years, the same three 3 percent were wealthier than the other ninety seven (97%) percent. In fact, they own most of the world. A goal is quantifiable wish with a timeline. A goal must be SMART.

S – Specific
M – Measurable
A – Attainable
R – Relevant
T– Time Oriented

You must determine what you want to achieve. Do not think about what you can or can not afford. Let your mind go wild. Sit in a quiet space and focus on your life over the next 30 years. Randomly write what comes to your mind.

Be outrageous. Be daring.

Become ridiculous. Have fun.

Write your 101 goals you desire to happen in your life. Don't think about how you are going to pay for them. Assume if you thought about them the universe will find a way to get them. Just think and write. Write down your first three experiences and any goals that attach to those experiences. Write goals and experiences you want to achieve over the next 30 years. Don't forget to include these categories:

Activities	Car	Career
Children	Housing	
Postsecondary/college	Stuff you like personally	

Be specific. If you desire to one day live in a 7000 square foot mansion decorated with Italian marble. Write it down. I have always wanted a Champagne Rolls Royce sitting in front of my vacation home in Monte Carlo, a Navy Blue Maserati at my Bermuda home and a motor boat at my private island in the Caribbean. Be specific.

Not sure what you want. Research magazines and the internet for what you want.

STOP

Do not read another page until the **101 Goals** list is complete. There is another copy in the appendix.

101 Goals

	Goal	**Goal Year**
1.		
2.		
3.		
4.		
5.		
6.		
7.		
8.		
9.		
10.		
11.		
12.		
13.		
14.		

15. _____ _____
16. _____ _____
17. _____ _____
18. _____ _____
19. _____ _____
20. _____ _____
21. _____ _____
22. _____ _____
23. _____ _____
24. _____ _____
25. _____ _____
26. _____ _____
27. _____ _____
28. _____ _____
29. _____ _____
30. _____ _____
31. _____ _____
32. _____ _____
33. _____ _____
34. _____ _____
35. _____ _____
36. _____ _____
37. _____ _____
38. _____ _____
39. _____ _____
40. _____ _____
41. _____ _____
42. _____ _____
43. _____ _____
44. _____ _____
45. _____ _____
46. _____ _____
47. _____ _____
48. _____ _____
49. _____ _____
50. _____ _____

51. _____ _____
52. _____ _____
53. _____ _____
54. _____ _____
55. _____ _____
56. _____ _____
57. _____ _____
58. _____ _____
59. _____ _____
60. _____ _____
61. _____ _____
62. _____ _____
63. _____ _____
64. _____ _____
65. _____ _____
66. _____ _____
67. _____ _____
68. _____ _____
69. _____ _____
70. _____ _____
71. _____ _____
72. _____ _____
73. _____ _____
74. _____ _____
75. _____ _____
76. _____ _____
77. _____ _____
78. _____ _____
79. _____ _____
80. _____ _____
81. _____ _____
82. _____ _____
83. _____ _____
84. _____ _____
85. _____ _____
86. _____ _____

87. _____ _____
88. _____ _____
89. _____ _____
90. _____ _____
91. _____ _____
92. _____ _____
93. _____ _____
94. _____ _____
95. _____ _____
96. _____ _____
97. _____ _____
98. _____ _____
99. _____ _____
100. _____ _____
101. _____ _____

Review your goals and then put a year when you would like to achieve the goal next to it. Rearrange your 101 goals by the year you plan to achieve them

101 Goals

Goals completed in 1 year

1. _____ _____
2. _____ _____
3. _____ _____
4. _____ _____
5. _____ _____
6. _____ _____
7. _____ _____
8. _____ _____
9. _____ _____
10. _____ _____

Goals completed in 5 years

11. _____ _____
12. _____ _____
13. _____ _____
14. _____ _____
15. _____ _____
16. _____ _____
17. _____ _____
18. _____ _____
19. _____ _____
20. _____ _____
21. _____ _____
22. _____ _____
23. _____ _____
24. _____ _____
25. _____ _____

Goals completed in 10 years

26. _____ _____
27. _____ _____
28. _____ _____
29. _____ _____
30. _____ _____
31. _____ _____
32. _____ _____
33. _____ _____
34. _____ _____
35. _____ _____
36. _____ _____
37. _____ _____
38. _____ _____
39. _____ _____
40. _____ _____
41. _____ _____

42. _____ _____
43. _____ _____
44. _____ _____

Goals completed in 15 years

45. _____ _____
46. _____ _____
47. _____ _____
48. _____ _____
49. _____ _____
50. _____ _____
51. _____ _____
52. _____ _____
53. _____ _____
54. _____ _____
55. _____ _____
56. _____ _____
57. _____ _____
58. _____ _____
59. _____ _____
60. _____ _____
61. _____ _____
62. _____ _____
63. _____ _____
64. _____ _____
65. _____ _____

Goals completed in 25 years

66. _____ _____
67. _____ _____
68. _____ _____
69. _____ _____
70. _____ _____

71. _____ _____
72. _____ _____
73. _____ _____
74. _____ _____
75. _____ _____
76. _____ _____
77. _____ _____
78. _____ _____
79. _____ _____
80. _____ _____
81. _____ _____
82. _____ _____
83. _____ _____
84. _____ _____
85. _____ _____

Goals completed in 30 years

86. _____ _____
87. _____ _____
88. _____ _____
89. _____ _____
90. _____ _____
91. _____ _____
92. _____ _____
93. _____ _____
94. _____ _____
95. _____ _____
96. _____ _____
97. _____ _____
98. _____ _____
99. _____ _____
100. _____ _____
101. _____ _____

CHAPTER 6   PASSION WITHIN

Rather than choose a career for money, choose a career that brings you passion. Most individuals spend three quarters of our waking hours in a career. If it brings you passion it brings you happiness. Aren't we all looking for happiness? Money is important, but it does not necessarily bring you happiness. When individuals find careers that give them passion, money flows to them effortlessly. They are able to stay committed to the career for long stretches of time through what would be considered pain and agony for other people. The long term commitment usually brings success.

"True passion goes beyond deep interest – it's a powerful emotion" [30]

Four ingredients are needed to create this emotion of passion.

Values   Interest   Skills   Ambition

VISA for short, is your passport to a fun filled career and life.[31]

Your career should:

- ➥ Align with what you value
- ➥ Be based in your interest
- ➥ Uses your skills
- ➥ Supports your ambitions

These four ingredients act like a fuel that, when applied to your work, combusts into an enthusiastic flame. The more fuel you throw on the fire *(the more the values, interest skills and ambitions are applied through your work)*, the larger the flame will be *(the more passion your work will give you.)*[32]

We have already defined your ambitions. The intense question is "What do you value?"

Values

Merriam-Webster dictionary defines values something you highly esteem and place great importance. Your personality gives clues to what you value. In his book, **Psychological Types** (published in 1921), Carl Gustav Jung states human behavior is predictable and understandable. People have preferences for how they think and feel. These preferences are the basis for how people work, play and relate to other people. What are your preferences? Do you know?

Take the quizzes below to determine your preferences. On each quiz, check each circle that has the answer that best suits you. Read the group of statements after the quiz.[33]

Which situation energizes you?

1. Which of the following do you prefer more?

☐   Large, high-energy groups with a lot of people and a lot of interaction

☐   Smaller groups with more one-on-one interaction

2. Which of the following do you prefer more?

☐   I am fine with being the center of attention and in fact, often enjoy it.

☐   I prefer to lay back and watch things without all eyes being on me.

3. When meeting someone for the first time, I typically prefer to do which choice more:

☐   Talking

☐   Listening

4. I need ample time alone in order to regroup and revitalize

myself:

☐   No

☐   Yes

5. Are you a natural conversationalist?

☐   Yes

☐   No

6. If a situation calls for contemplation, do you typically prefer to:

☐   Talk it out with others

☐   Think about the situation alone

7. When you think of your ideal day, is the majority of that time spent:

☐   With a lot of people

☐   Alone and/or with a few others

8. Do you typically:

☐   Tolerate large crowds most of the time as long as it isn't thwarting progress in some kind of way

☐   Dislike large crowds in most scenarios

9. I am more:

☐   Outward

☐   Inward

10. I enjoy and look forward to situations where I can meet new people.

☐   Yes

☐   No

11. I like to get involved with social activities.

☐   Yes

☐   No

12. If I have free time, I generally like to spend it with others.

☐   Yes

☐   No

13. I look forward to and look to get involved with social events.

☐   Yes

☐   No

14. If involved with group activity and group involvement, I'm at my best if I can take private breaks for myself.

☐   No

☐   Yes

15. After prolonged social activities, I prefer to spend some time by myself, away from socializing.

☐   No

☐   Yes

If you answer more than 8 of the top answers, then your **Energy Preference** is that of being extroverted, meaning you gain energy from their direct involvement with people and the outside world. For the sake of this book we will refer to your energy capacity as **E**.

If you answer less than 8 of the bottom answers, then **Energy Preference** is that of being introverted, meaning you gain energy when given the opportunity to spend time alone and think things through. For the sake of this book we will refer to your energy capacity as **I**.

Energy Characteristics - EXTROVERTED

- Doesn't mind being in large groups and often enjoys it
- Likes to know and associate with lots of people
- Prefers social interaction to time alone
- When confronted with a problem, typically likes to talk it out with others and get their point of view
- Known to speak before thinking

- Doesn't typically have trouble thinking of something to say, and is typically at ease in doing so
- Doesn't typically have problems meeting new people wherever they go
- Listening more difficult than talking
- Easily adapts to social situations
- Typically appreciates situations for what they are worth as they are happening
- After attending a party you have enormous energy
- Read or have conversation with radio or TV in background
- Telephone call welcome interruptions

Energy Characteristics - INTROVERTED

- Prefers one-on-one to large-group interaction
- Prefers to have a few close relationships
- Needs time alone to restore energy
- Typically good listeners
- More likely to think before speaking than extraverts are
- May be lost for words at times, not knowing what to say
- Enjoys reflecting
- May need to get time to self to take things in before fully appreciating them
- Dislikes crowds
- Reserved sometimes shy
- Rehearses everything before speaking
- High concentration to shut out background distractions

Please note your personality can have both energy characteristics. The question is which one is your dominant preference. While E's are the social type, some I's are quite social. The difference is what happens after socializing. E's are charged and look for more social time with others. I's need some alone time to recharge. Both may be great speakers and conversationalist, but the source of their energy may be different.

Circle your Energy Preference

E or I

How do you Process Information?

1. Which kind of world would you prefer to live in?

☐   A world with endless possibilities that enlighten, and where change takes place often

☐   A solid, realistic, tangible world based on what is known

2. Which do you typically prefer to think about?

☐   New experiences

☐   Same reliable experiences

3. Do you consider yourself to be good with vision and seeing long-term?

☐   Yes

☐   No

4. Do you often think of things that others often don't?

☐   Yes

☐   No

5. I trust what I know and what I see.

☐   No

☐   Yes

6. Do you find yourself thinking about the future often?

☐   Yes

☐   No

7. Which do you find yourself focused on?

☐   Possibilities

☐   What exists

8. Which do you prefer?

☐   Introspection

☐   Observation

9. In comparison to others, my strengths are in my:

☐ Imagination, creativity, innovation

☐ Sound grasp of reality and how things are done

10. Are you:

☐ Absent-minded

☐ Typically firmly planted in the moment and aware of conventions

11. Which statement below describes you best?

☐ I often don't take note of customary norms, tradition, ritual, and the conventional way things are done, and am often thinking of other things.

☐ I easily grasp these things.

12. Some people may consider me to be absent-minded.

☐ Yes

☐ No

13. I am:

☐ Losing touch of my surroundings as I think of other things

☐ In touch with my surroundings

14. I am complex.

☐ Yes

☐ No

15. I am more:

☐ Theoretical and conceptual

☐ Concrete and empirical

16. Are you more likely to:

☐ See how something fits into the big picture and see how it is related to other things

☐ Notice and absorb details

17. I find myself typically coming to conclusions:

☐ In a jumping-about fashion

☐ On a step-by-step basis

18. Do you:

☐ Hope to apply the information to a larger context

☐ Take information for what its worth

19. Do you prefer to:

☐ Come to new conclusions

☐ Stick with proven, reliable conclusions

20. I like to think about how things can be improved:

☐ Yes

☐ No

21. I can often tell what someone is going to say after a few sentences:

☐ Yes

☐ No

22. I like to think about new ways of doing things.

☐ Yes

☐ No

23. I like to think of ways to expand and improve things.

☐ Yes

☐ No

24. I have a vivid imagination that I like to exercise.

☐ Yes

☐ No

25. I prefer to:

☐ Speak in generalities

☐   Speak in specifics

26. I trust my experiences and consider them to be reliable in making my decisions

☐   No

☐   Yes

If you select 12 or more of the bottom answers your **Process Information Preference** is that of being Sensing, meaning you rely on your senses to process information. You rely on what is, what exists, facts figures. You take in information literally and catch most of the nuances and details that others miss. For the sake of this book, we will refer to your process information capacity as **S**.

If you select 14 or more of the top answers your **Process Information Preference** is that of being Intuitive, meaning you rely on what could be to process information. You compare and apply that information to some type of larger, big picture context - thinking of underlying meanings, envisioning possibilities, and intuiting what these can tell us about the future. You rely on your imagination, hunches and new ideas. For the sake of this book we will refer to your process information capacity as **N**.

Process Information Characteristics - SENSING

- ➜   Good with the concrete (what can be seen)
- ➜   Likes to think about what exists
- ➜   Realistic
- ➜   Typically has plenty of common sense
- ➜   Pays attention to and remembers details
- ➜   Takes in information in a step-by-step manner
- ➜   Prefers direct experience
- ➜   Pays attention to their surroundings
- ➜   "I like to focus on the present and what exists in front of me."

Process Information Characteristics - INTUITIVE

- ➜   Good with the abstract

- Likes to think of what's possible
- Has an active imagination
- Thinks outside the box
- Enjoys seeing things in different ways
- Likes to daydream
- May be difficult to understand
- May have unexplainable hunches or a sixth sense
- Gets motivated by their inspirations
- "I like to think about the future and what it could or may hold."

Please note your personality can have both process information characteristics. Which one is your dominant preference?

Circle your Process Information Preference

S or N

How do you make decisions?

1. Which do you value you more?

☐ Truth

☐ Harmony

2. You would rather:

☐ Understand the reason behind where someone is coming from

☐ Understand the emotions that someone is coming from

3. Which do you prefer?

☐ Justice

☐ Compassion

4. I typically make decisions with my:

☐ Head

☐ Heart

5. In a disagreement I am more likely to concede to another if

☐ I find that my reasoning was incorrect

☐ I find that we need to get along

6. Which is more important to you?

☐ Logic

☐ Feelings

7. I am more:

☐ Hardnosed, rational, blunt

☐ Forgiving, compassionate, tactful

8. When I help people with their problems, my strength is in:

☐ Figuring out what went wrong and how to fix it

☐ Providing emotional support and helping them feel better

9. I am more:

☐ Analytical

☐ Empathetic

10. When others speak I find myself:

☐ Being critical, looking to find inconsistencies

☐ Looking to find reasons for support and appreciation

11. I make decisions based on:

☐ Objective logic

☐ Personal values

12. Which do you prefer?

☐ If something makes sense

☐ If something feels right

13. I am more:

☐ Tough-minded

☐ Sentimental

14. Objective criticism should be practiced more often:

☐ Yes

☐ No

15. I find that sentimental moments and activities are special and mean a lot to me.

☐ No

☐ Yes

16. Which is more like you?

☐ I am eager to help others understand and realize things

☐ I am eager to help others feel better

17. When in a disagreement with someone, you typically:

☐ Try to find the truth in the matter (get to the bottom and solve the problem)

☐ Try to find reason for a mutual agreement and common ground

18. It is important to me that everyone gets along.

☐ No

☐ Yes

If you select 10 or more of the top answers your **Decision Making Preference** is that of Thinking, meaning you prefer to make decisions objectively with your head, through logic. You value justice and fairness. For the sake of this book we will refer to your Decision Making capacity as **T**.

If you select 9 or more of the bottom answers your **Decision Making Preference** is that of Feeling, meaning you prefer to make decisions subjectively, with you heart, based on emotion.

You value harmony and empathy. For the sake of this book we will refer to your Decision Making capacity as **F**.

Please note your personality can have both decision making characteristics. Which one is your dominant preference?

Decision Making Characteristics - THINKING

- Wants truth and justice
- Hard-nosed, firm
- Decides with head
- Naturally skeptical
- Critical
- Blunt
- Looks at principles
- Objective
- "There is a principle and outcome to everything."

Decision Making Characteristics - FEELING

- Naturally sympathetic
- Strives for harmony
- Empathetic and forgiving
- Decides with heart
- Naturally trusts others
- Supportive
- Tactful
- Concerned with the feelings of others
- "There is a human element to everything."

Circle your Decision Making Preference

T or F

How do you choose to live your life?

1. I prefer to:

☐ Come to conclusions about things

☐ Keep things open-ended

2. I prefer:

☐ Standard, familiar, predictable procedure

☐ To be flexible and adaptable

3. I am typically comfortable making decisions.

☐ Yes

☐ No

4. When in the process of coming to a conclusion I typically:

☐ Like to come to a quick conclusion and go with it

☐ Take things in and may wait before jumping to my conclusion

5. Is your first reaction to consult directions if they are recommended or available?

☐ Yes

☐ No

6. I typically:

☐ Like to know what I'm doing ahead of time and plan things out

☐ Like to be spontaneous and take things as they come

7. I am good at:

☐ Preparing and scheduling

☐ Improvisation and adaptation

8. I am:

☐ Structured

☐ Spontaneous

9. If working on a project or assignment I am likely to:

- ☐ Try to get it done (at least a good portion of it) before the last minute
- ☐ Wait until close to a deadline to really focus on something and get it done

10. I prefer:

- ☐ A few clear, definite options
- ☐ Many broad, changeable options

11. I prefer to:

- ☐ Plan ahead
- ☐ Wait and see what comes up

12. I prefer:

- ☐ Situations that are in control
- ☐ Situations allowing freedom

13. I make ?To do? lists and follow them.

- ☐ Yes
- ☐ No

14. I enjoy the following more:

- ☐ Finishing assignments or projects
- ☐ Starting assignments or projects

15. I naturally will take responsibility and prepare to get something done.

- ☐ Yes
- ☐ No

16. I am a creature of habit.

- ☐ Yes
- ☐ No

17. I feel that most of my time needs to have purpose.

☐　Yes

☐　No

18. I value the process and intrinsic value of doing things more than the final outcome.

☐　No

☐　Yes

19. I am more likely to:

☐　Work on one thing at a time, making sure that it gets finished

☐　Start a few things during a period of time

Lifestyle Orientation Characteristics- JUDGING

- ➜ Likes to plan
- ➜ Organized
- ➜ Likes to come to conclusions
- ➜ Prepared
- ➜ Enjoys finishing things
- ➜ Relies on schedules, to-do lists, and deadlines
- ➜ Don't Like Surprises
- ➜ Sees and sets boundaries
- ➜ Values a job well done
- ➜ Likes to know what to expect ahead of time
- ➜ Decisive
- ➜ Always waiting on others
- ➜ Have everything in place

Lifestyle Orientation Characteristics- PERCEIVING

- ➜ Likes options
- ➜ Places emphasis on having fun
- ➜ Spontaneous
- ➜ Delays decision-making
- ➜ Flexible
- ➜ Good with improvisation
- ➜ Adapts, goes with the flow

- Enjoys starting things
- Can work on many things at once
- Enjoys surprises
- Doesn't like to commit because they never know what may come up

If you select 10 or more of the top answers your **Lifestyle Orientation Preference** is that of Judging, meaning you prefer to plan things out and live in a structured manner. For the sake of this book we will refer to your Lifestyle Orientation capacity as **J**.

If you select 10 or more of the bottom answers your **Lifestyle Orientation Preference** is that of Perceiving, meaning you prefer to make decisions subjectively, with you heart, based on emotion. You value harmony and empathy. For the sake of this book we will refer to your Lifestyle Orientation capacity as **P**.

Please note your personality can have both decision making characteristics. Which one is your dominant preference?

Circle your Lifestyle Orientation Preference

J or P

CHAPTER 7   YOUR PERSONALITY TYPE

Place all four of your preference symbols here. In the order indicated.

Energy	Process Information	Decision Making	Lifestyle Orientation

These four preferences are considered your personality type. Certain personalities gravitate toward certain careers. Rather than looking at a career just to earn money look at it as your life passion at work. Let's see what careers does your personality type gravitate to and famous people you resemble.

These personality types, discovered by Carl Jung, are called Myers- Briggs Type Indicators (MBTI) ® [34] There are 16 personality types. There is a description of each personality type, a career list, famous people with same personality type and a picture of fictional characters with the same personality type. Watch one of these shows/films and study the character's personality.

ENFJ   Smooth Talking Persuaders

Extravert, iNtuitive, Feeling, Judging – ENFJ personalities represent approximately 5% of the population. ENFJs actively care about people in an intense manner and they have a strong desire to bring harmony into their relationships. They are empathetic, intuitive, warm, enthusiastic, compassionate, responsible, and idealistic. They have a clear sense of right and wrong and

Russell in *Disney's UP*

they share this openly with others. They draw conclusions about people they interact with quickly and with certainty and it is difficult for them to change these perceptions, good or bad, once the conclusion has been drawn. They would be best in, and need, a career in which they will work with people and be able to make decisions based on their personal values. A career that makes good use of their organizational skills, breadth of interests, their grasp of possibilities, and their warmth and sympathy, would be an interesting and satisfying choice for ENFJs.

"A small group of thoughtful people could change the world. Indeed, it's the only thing that ever has."

Margaret Mead

ENFJs are people-focused individuals. They live in the world of people possibilities. More so than any other type, they have excellent people skills. They understand and care about people, and have a special talent for bringing out the best in others. Their main interest in life is giving love, support, and a good time to other people. They naturally lead and direct others, seeking and finding their strengths and helping mold those strengths into action with their enthusiasm and supporting nature. In short, they have a real knack for bringing out the best in others.

Bilbo Baggins from *The Hobbit* and *Lord of the Rings*

"If not me, who? And if not now, when?"

Mikhail Gorbachev

Because it is so important that other people like them, ENFJs are outgoing, friendly, and genuinely concerned about the welfare of others and they try to handle things with regard for other people's feelings. They tend to be rather idealistic and use their personal values to rule their lives. They are caring, warm, and enthusiastic people, with great energy for projects or causes they believe in.

Natural leaders, ENFJs, are usually able to communicate in ways that make others feel excited about their ideas and they are social, popular, and active in a variety of settings. They can make just about anything sound good. Persuading others is not hard for them to do. Yet, ENFJ's are also great diplomats and are known for their great consideration and tact. They work hard to develop and maintain harmony in all their relationships. ENFJs are intrigued with new possibilities, especially those that make positive changes, help other people, or generally make the world a better place.

An ENFJs Career Choice Should Probably Include...

1. A supportive and friendly environment where they work with people they trust and like, and where they feel appreciated for their efforts.
2. The opportunity to work with groups, feel challenged, and be able to meet new people and develop warm, long-term relationships.
3. A career that offers responsibility and the chance to fulfill their humanitarian values.
4. The chance to utilize their curiosity for ideas and think about possibilities and work on creative solutions to problems that will help others or improve the quality of life.
5. The ability to work on many interesting projects, use their great organizational skills, and maintain a high degree of control and responsibility.
6. The opportunity to speak and develop leader ship roles

FAMOUS PEOPLE ~ ENFJ PERSONALITY TYPE

Do you know what contributions these people provided to the world? If not, look up their names as discover their impact.

Martin Luther King	Ralph Nader
Billy Graham	Heraldo Rivera
Margaret Mead	Mikhail Gorbachev

ENFP   Creative Enthusiast

Extravert, i**N**tuitive, **F**eeling, **P**erceiving – ENFP personalities represent approximately 5% of the population. ENFP's have an independent nature and original minds, yet are people-friendly, and receptive to the needs of others. ENFPs are enthusiastic, charming, ingenuous, imaginative, risk-taking, sensitive, people-oriented individuals with capabilities ranging across a broad spectrum. Most ENFPs have good people skills and place great importance on their interpersonal relationships. They almost always have a strong need to be liked. They excel at bringing out the best in others, and

Sponge Bob

are typically well-liked for this reason. They have an exceptional ability to intuitively understand a person after a very short period of time, and use their intuition and flexibility to relate to others on their own level. For ENFPs, details of everyday life are seen as trivial drudgery. They place no importance on detailed, maintenance-type tasks and will frequently remain oblivious to these types of concerns. When they do have to perform these tasks, they do not enjoy themselves. They have the ability to be productive with little supervision, as long as they are excited about what they're doing.

> *"Life was meant to be lived, and curiosity must be kept alive."*
>
> Eleanor Roosevelt

ENFPs have an unusually broad range of skills and talents. They are good at most things which interest them. To onlookers, the ENFP may seem directionless and without purpose, but ENFPs are actually quite consistent. They yearn to get the most out of life. They enhance life, trying to get the most out of experiences and emotion. They have a spark about them. Something that others feel, but can't explain. They are truly independent individuals, often looked up to by others, often with their acquaintances walking away feeling better about themselves. They have a laid-back, stylish, enjoyable demeanor that is often seen as being creatively cool and charismatic.

> *"I feel that luck is preparation meeting opportunity"*
>
> Oprah Winfrey

ENFPs are good at a lot of different things. An ENFP can generally achieve a good degree of success at anything which has interested him or her. ENFPs are warm, enthusiastic people, typically very bright and full of potential. ENFPs are extremely open-minded. They live in the world of possibilities, and can become very passionate and excited about things. Their enthusiasm lends them the ability to inspire and motivate others, more so than we see in other types. They can talk their way in, or out, of anything. They love life, seeing it as a special gift, and strive to make the most out of it.

"Marching to the beat of a different drummer" is a hallmark trait of ENFPs and they admire others who are of the same mind. This quality allows them to be a driving force and make things happen. This is both a strength and a weakness. Used productively, this trait allows them to be a unique type of worker who can take a minimum of instruction and use his/her natural talents to expand on ideas and

Raven in
That's So Raven

concepts and produce a finished product that goes above and beyond what was expected. The downside is that this trait can also stop an ENFP from producing anything of value. If he/she feels the instructions and work assigned goes against his/her value system, an ENFP can "stonewall" production by being obstinate and confrontational in expressing concerns over the "right and wrong" aspects.

An ENFPs Career Choice Should Probably Include...

1. A position where they are not confined by strict schedules, mundane tasks, rules, regulations or restrictions.
2. A creative, fun, relaxed and easy going environment where they can work with a variety of people each day.
3. A place where they have a lot of flexibility, and where they can work with people and ideas.
4. Plenty of opportunities to be challenged by new situations, where each day is different from the day before.
5. The ability to talk about ideas, possibilities, and implications and then see their innovations become a reality.
6. The chance to make a difference and work on projects they believe in.

FAMOUS PEOPLE ~ ENFJ PERSONALITY TYPE
Do you know what contributions these people provided to the world? If not, look up their names as discover their impact.

Oprah Winfrey   Barack Obama
Adam Sandler   Cher
Bill Cosby   Dr. Seuss
Eleanor Roosevelt   Dave Arquette

ENTJ   Life's Natural Leaders

Extravert, iNtuitive, Thinking, Judging – ENFT personalities represent approximately 5% of the population. ENTJs are natural born leaders. They live in a world of possibilities where they see all sorts challenges to be surmounted, and they want to be the ones responsible for surmounting them. They make decisions quickly, and are quick to verbalize their opinions and decisions to the rest of the world. ENTJs love to interact

Ben Tennyson in
Ben 10

with people. As Extroverts, they're energized and stimulated primarily externally. There's nothing more enjoyable and satisfying to the ENTJ than having a lively, challenging conversation. They especially respect people who are able to stand up to the ENTJ, and argue persuasively for their point of view. There aren't too many people who will do so, however, because the ENTJ is a very forceful and dynamic presence who has a tremendous amount of self-confidence and excellent verbal communication skills. Even the most confident individuals may experience moments of self-doubt when debating a point with an ENTJ.

"Control your own destiny or someone else will."

Jack Welch

ENTJs are very career-focused, and fit into the corporate world quite naturally. They are constantly scanning their environment for potential problems which they can turn into solutions. They

Hermone from The
Harry Potter

generally see things from a long-range perspective, and are usually successful at identifying plans to turn problems around - especially problems of a corporate nature. ENTJs are usually successful in the business world, because they are so driven to leadership. They're tireless in their efforts on the job, and driven to visualize where an organization is headed. For these reasons, they are natural corporate leaders.

"Being prime minister is a lonely job... you cannot lead from the crowd"

Margaret Thatcher

ENTJs are friendly, energetic people who like to be in charge and make things happen. They are strong willed decision makers who are good at seeing the logical consequences of their choices. They tend to be organized and logical in their approach to all situations, readily seeing and correcting flaws in organizations and systems. ENTJs love challenges and face problems head on. They strive to be competent in all they do and enjoy learning new things and adding to their impressive store of knowledge.

Leonardo in *Teenage Mutant Ninja Turtles*

Good leaders and communicators, ENTJs command respect from those around them and are able to express their long range vision to others. They value honesty, so they are truthful and direct. ENTJs often know a lot of people and enjoy making connections between unrelated parties to bring about change and improvement in their communities.

An ENTJs Career Choice Should Probably Include...

1. An environment where respect for contributions of ideas and actions is acknowledged and appreciated.
2. The chance to be a leader while interacting with a variety of people on a variety of projects throughout the day.
3. The chance to develop strategies that will perfect or improve the efficiency of systems.
4. Work that lets them solve complex problems in creative yet logical ways, working with other people they respect.
5. A position that does not require them to be sensitive to the spiritual, emotional, or personal needs of others.
6. A competitive structured and organized work environment where evaluation and compensation is done in a fair and consistent manner.

FAMOUS PEOPLE ~ ENTJ PERSONALITY TYPE
Do you know what contributions these people provided to the world? If not, look up their names as discover their impact.

Jack Welch   Margaret Thatcher
Al Sharpton   Tammy Bruce
Bill Gates   Dr. Phil

ENTP   The Visionary Inventors

Bugs Bunny

Extravert, i**N**tuitive, **T**hinking, **P**erceiving – ENTP personalities represent approximately 5% of the population. ENTPs are exciting, enthusiastic, friendly, amusing, outgoing, and talkative people. They generally understand things quickly and with great depth, allowing them to be flexible and adapt well to a wide range of tasks. ENTPs are visionaries and their perceptive abilities allow them to see possibilities everywhere. They get excited and enthusiastic about their ideas, and are able to spread their enthusiasm to others. However, they are less interested in developing plans of action or making decisions than they are in generating possibilities and ideas. Following through on the implementation of an idea is usually a chore to the ENTP. They are fluent conversationalists, mentally quick, and enjoy verbal sparring with others. They love to debate issues, and may even switch sides sometimes just for the love of the debate.

"It's kind of fun to do the impossible."

Walt Disney

Although the ENTP is more interested in absorbing information than in making decisions, they are quite rational and logical in reaching conclusions. When they apply Thinking to their Intuitive perceptions, the outcome can be very powerful indeed. A well-developed ENTP is extremely visionary, inventive, and enterprising.

Fat Albert

ENTPs are characterized by a quick ingenuity. They are clever and amusing, constantly scanning for the new and unusual around them. They are very perceptive and notice possibilities everywhere. ENTPs are resourceful in making what they imagine become a reality. They are impulsive and versatile, love surprises, and are adaptable to change. They are pragmatic, goal-oriented, and creative problem-solvers and can be especially good at using their charm and wit to inspire others and enroll them into their own endeavors. They are great public speakers. They are natural leaders who are logical, rational thinkers.

"The attitude is we live and let live."

Tom Wolfe

Garfield

ENTPs are able to weigh the cause and effect of various choices and critique several options at once due to their propensity for logical thinking. They are often energetic conversationalists and thoroughly enjoy debating issues. An ENTP will sometimes argue for the sake of argument, simply for the enjoyment they receive from the interplay of ideas with another person. Spontaneous and easy going, they look for fun in everything they do and bring zest and originality to every project.

An ENTPs Career Choice Should Probably Include...

1. An opportunity to further develop their introverted thinking to help them critique their ideas and inspirations.
2. The opportunity to work on a variety of creative challenges that let them try new and different approaches.
3. A casual yet exciting atmosphere where rules and restrictions are kept to a minimum.
4. An environment that encourages and condones risk-taking and autonomy.

5. Plenty of opportunities to meet influential people and constantly increase their own level of personal power.
6. The chance to be recognized, evaluated, and compensated for their creativity, expertise, and competence and to see their visions materialized into the world.

FAMOUS PEOPLE ~ ENTP PERSONALITY TYPE
Do you know what contributions these people provided to the world? If not, look up their names as discover their impact.

Walt Disney
Andy Roddick
Ashton Kutcher

Warren Bennis
Christopher Columbus
Tom Wolfe

ESFJ — Hosts/ Hostess to the World

Extravert, **S**ensing, **F**eeling, **J**udging – ESFJ personalities represent approximately 13% of the population. ESFJs are people persons - they love people. They are warmly interested in others and are compassionate, conscientious, cooperative, loyal, opinionated, personable, and responsible people. They use their Sensing and Judging characteristics to gather specific, detailed information about others, and turn this information into supportive judgments. They want to like people, and have a special skill at bringing out the best in others. They are extremely good at reading others, and understanding their point of view. The ESFJ's strong desire to be liked and for everything to be pleasant makes them highly supportive of others. People like to be around ESFJs, because the ESFJ has a special gift for making people feel good about themselves.

> Lois Griffin
> in *The Family Guy*

"There are no regrets in life, just lessons."

Jennifer Aniston

ESFJs are warm and energetic. They need approval from others to feel good about themselves. They are hurt by indifference and don't understand unkindness. They are very giving people, who get a lot of their personal satisfaction from the happiness of others. They want to be appreciated for who they are, and what they give. They're very sensitive to others, and freely give practical care. ESFJs are such caring individuals, that they sometimes have a hard time seeing or accepting a difficult truth about someone they care about.

"If I judge a character, I'm defeating the purpose.."

Danny Glover

ESFJs enjoy meeting and helping people and are friendly, outgoing, and talkative. They place a high value on relationships, are very concerned with the feelings of others and eager to please in real and tangible ways. They are sympathetic and caring people, with strong opinions based on their values. Often popular, they have great energy for their many projects, activities, and friends.

Eddie in
That's So Raven

ESFJs have great common sense and good minds and memories for details, especially those that relate to people. They are hard working, organized, and conscientious, liking best to be part of a cooperative team. Rather traditional by nature, they are willing to put large amounts of energy into the things they believe in and faithfully follow through on all their commitments.

An ESFJs Career Choice Should Probably Include...

1. An opportunity in which they can use their skills to manipulate facts and details.

2. A stable, traditional environment, harmonious and cooperative where they feel appreciated for their hard work and contributions and where they feel part of a caring team.
3. An opportunity to influence others and help others find and develop their strengths.
4. Explicit and clear rules, regulation, and expectation where they know their responsibilities and are compensated for what they produce.
5. Work that lets them see the tangible results of their efforts and has a direct and positive effect on people.
6. The chance to learn and master the skills of their trade, and organize and retain control over their projects.

FAMOUS PEOPLE ~ ESFJ PERSONALITY TYPE
Do you know what contributions these people provided to the world? If not, look up their names as discover their impact.

Regis Philbin
Jennifer Aniston
William McKinley

George Washington
Donny Osmond
Danny Glover

ESFP   You Only Go Around Once

The Donkey in *Shrek*

Extravert, Sensing, Feeling, Perceiving – ESFP personalities represent approximately 13% of the population. ESFPs have very strong interpersonal skills, and may frequently find themselves in the role of the peacemaker. They are easy, outgoing, friendly, accepting, unprejudiced, open-minded, and tolerant people who rely on their direct senses. Since they make decisions by using their personal values, they are usually very sympathetic and concerned for other people's well-being. They're usually quite generous and warm. They are very observant about other people, and seem to sense what is wrong with someone before others might, responding warmly with a solution to a practical need. They might not be the best advice-givers in the world, because they dislike theory and future-planning, but they are great for giving practical care.

"Reality is wrong. Dreams are for real."

TuPac Shakur

ESFPs are spontaneous, optimistic individuals. They love to have fun so much that they can become overindulgent and place more importance on immediate sensation and gratification than on their duties and obligations. They may also avoid looking at long-term consequences of their actions. For the ESFP, the entire world is a stage. They love to be the center of attention and perform for people. They're constantly putting on a show for others to entertain them and make them happy. They enjoy stimulating other people's senses, and are extremely good at it. They would love nothing more than for life to be a continual party, in which they play the role of the fun-loving host.

"The way I see it, you should live everyday like it's your birthday."

Paris Hilton

Eikichi Onizuka in
Great Teacher
Onizuka

ESFPs are friendly, warm, and energetic people who usually have a wide and varied circle of friends. They are active, talkative, and easy going with a love of life that is infectious to everyone around them. They look for and find fun in everything they do and are at their best when they are busy doing things with people they enjoy. Realistic, sensible, and down to earth, ESFPs are good with details, and have great memories for the facts that pertain to people.

"La vida loca, that's my life right now."

Ricky Martin

Sympathetic and eager to help anyone, ESFPs are usually not interested in judging or trying to control others. Many ESFPs have a great love of animals and nature. Using their well developed common sense, they are usually good at solving immediate problems to make things easier or make a real and tangible   difference in people's lives. Their spontaneity and adaptability enable them to respond quickly to opportunities and keep several balls in the air at one time.

An ESFPs Career Choice Should Probably Include...

1. Plenty of opportunities to work closely with a variety of other people on a variety of projects throughout the day.
2. The opportunity to use their great people skills and practical perspective, which will also provide them with enough new challenges that they will not become bored.
3. A relaxed, friendly, and active environment where they feel part of a team and they are appreciated and rewarded for there contributions.
4. Work that is of a practical and helpful nature, where they have plenty of hands-on involvement and are able to see the results of their efforts.
5. The opportunity to learn and master skills and then use them to solve problems using their common sense and realistic point of view.
6. The chance to mediate problems, solve crises, and use their warmth and sense of humor to defuse difficult or tense situations and bring them to positive endings.

FAMOUS PEOPLE ~ ESFP PERSONALITY TYPE
Do you know what contributions these people provided to the world? If not, look up their names as discover their impact.

Bill Clinton
Brittany Spears
Marilyn Monroe
Ricky Martin

Paris Hilton
Magic Johnson
Paula Abdul
TuPac Shakur

Lil Kim   Miley Cyrus

ESTJ   Life's Administrators

Extravert, Sensing, Thinking, Judging – ESTJ personalities represent approximately 13% of the population. ESTJs live in the present world with a focus on facts and concrete needs. They are aggressive, analytic, conscientious, decisive and direct, efficient, fact-minded individuals. ESTJs are constantly scanning their personal environment to make sure that everything is running smoothly and systematically. They have a clear set of standards and beliefs and honor traditions and laws. They expect the same of others, and have no patience or understanding of individuals who do not value these systems. ESTJs like to see quick results for their efforts and they value competence and efficiency.

"Success is the result of perfection, hard work, learning from failure, loyalty, and persistence."

Colin Powell

Clair Huxtable in
The Cosby Show

ESTJs are take-charge people, with a clear vision of the way that things should be, and leadership roles come naturally. They are self-confident and aggressive, talented at devising systems and plans for action, and at being able to see what steps need to be taken to complete a specific task. They can sometimes be very demanding and critical and they are likely to express themselves without reserve if they feel someone isn't meeting their standards. ESTJs are straightforward and honest and can be taken at face-value.

ESTJs are friendly, outgoing, and honest. They tend to be traditional and conservative in their views and are comfortable expressing their opinions. Because ESTJs trust their own personal experiences, they are most interested in working with real things, and solving immediate problems rather than dealing with theory or possibilities. Usually well-organized and efficient, ESTJs work hard to meet or exceed the expectations others have for them. They are practical and realistic and want everything to make sense and be in order.

"We must stop thinking of the individual and start thinking about what is best for society"

Hillary Clinton

ESTJs are direct and frank, liking to get busy, stay busy, and have a lot to show for their efforts. Using logic to draw their conclusions, ESTJs like to make decisions and get on with their next project. Responsible and conscientious, they enjoy being in charge and therefore are usually great

Mufasa in *The Lion King*

managers, able to keep others organized and on track.

An ESTJs Career Choice Should Probably Include...

1. Work that takes into account their breadth of interests, reliance on facts, and their logical and analytical thinking patterns.
2. An organized and efficient environment with explicit rules and expectations and standards to follow.
3. A busy, active yet predictable workplace, where they work with many different people throughout the day in a team environment
4. The opportunity to hold a high level of responsibility, and grow into a leadership role.
5. An opportunity to work with like minded people to create order and structure in their environment.

6. Work that is of a practical nature, where they can see the results of their work and where their contributions are measured in fair, logical ways.

FAMOUS PEOPLE ~ ESTJ PERSONALITY TYPE
Do you know what contributions these people provided to the world? If not, look up their names as discover their impact.

Bill O'Reilly
Colin Powell
Mitt Romney

Judge Judy
Hillary Clinton

ESTP   The Ultimate Realist

Extravert, **S**ensing, **T**hinking, **P**erceiving – ESTP personalities represent approximately 13% of the population. ESTPs are outgoing, straight-shooting types. Enthusiastic and excitable, ESTPs are "doers" who live in the world of action. Blunt, straightforward risk-takers, they are willing to plunge right into things and get their hands dirty. They live in the here-and-now, and place little importance on introspection or theory. The look at the facts of a situation, quickly decide what should be done, execute the action, and move on to the next thing.

"It's okay to be crazy, but don't be insane."

P. Diddy

ESTPs have an uncanny ability to perceive people's attitudes and motivations. They pick up on little cues which go completely unnoticed by most other types, such as facial expressions and stance. They're typically a couple of steps ahead of the person they're interacting with. ESTPs use this ability to get what they want out of a situation. Rules and laws are seen as guidelines for behavior, rather than mandates. If the ESTP has decided that something

Ursula in *The Little Mermaid*

needs to be done, then their "do it and get on with it" attitude takes precedence over the rules. However, the ESTP tends to have their own strong belief in what's right and what's wrong, and will doggedly stick to their principles. The Rules of the Establishment may hold little value to the ESTP, but their own integrity mandates that they will not under any circumstances do something which they feel to be wrong.

"You get what you give. What you put into things is what you get out of them."

Jennifer Lopez

Spontaneous and playful, ESTPs enjoy being at the center of attention and are often the life of a party. They are good at noticing the specific details of any situation, sizing up a problem and then quickly responding to it. They are better at immediate rather than long range problem solving. ESTPs can be good negotiators and tough, logical decision-makers when necessary but they prefer a "live and let live" attitude and lifestyle.

"As long as your going to be thinking anyway, think big."

Donald Trump

Alvin in *The Chipmunks*

ESTPs are friendly, energetic, and active people with great powers of observation and the ability to be completely in the moment at all times. They are realistic, curious, and pragmatic, tending to speak directly and clearly without worrying about hidden meanings or ulterior motives. ESTPs are usually easygoing but can be firm believers in taking responsibility for one self. They tend to like activities that are active and physical in nature and enjoy a certain amount of risk taking.

An ESTPs Career Choice Should Probably Include...

1. The opportunity to have personal and direct involvement with projects where they can see the tangible results of their efforts.
2. The freedom to work in a relaxed and friendly environment with opportunities to interact throughout the day with a variety of different people.
3. An environment where they are in charge of their time and responsible for their actions with a minimum of rules and restrictions.
4. A constantly changing and interesting environment with plenty of excitement.
5. The opportunity to use logical reasoning to determine the best and most efficient solutions to tactical problems.
6. Challenging, fun ways to demonstrate their abilities to respond to immediate challenges.

FAMOUS PEOPLE ~ ESTP PERSONALITY TYPE
Do you know what contributions these people provided to the world? If not, look up their names as discover their impact.

Kobe Bryant	P-Diddy Combs
Kid Rock	Shaquille O'Neil
Arnold Schwarzenegger	Madonna
John F. Kennedy	Jennifer Lopez
Muhammad Ali	Donald Trump

INFJ   The Counselor

Introvert, iNtuitive, Feeling, Judging – INFJ personalities represent approximately 1% of the population. INFJs place great importance on having things orderly and systematic in their outer world. They put a lot of energy into identifying the best system for getting things done, and constantly define and redefine the priorities in their lives. On the other hand, INFJs operate within themselves on an intuitive basis which is entirely spontaneous. They know things intuitively, without being able to pinpoint why, and without detailed knowledge of the subject at hand. They are usually right, and they usually know it. Consequently, INFJs put a tremendous amount of faith into their instincts and intuitions. This is something of a conflict between the inner and outer worlds, and may result in the INFJ not being as organized as other Judging types tend to be. Or we may see some signs of disarray in an otherwise orderly tendency, such as a consistently messy desk.

> *"The hunger for love is much more difficult to remove than the hunger for bread.""*

> Mother Teresa

INFJs have uncanny insight into people and situations. They get "feelings" about things and intuitively understand them. As an extreme example, some of them report experiences of a psychic nature, such as getting strong feelings about there being a problem with a loved one, and discovering later that they were in a car accident. This is the sort of thing that other types may scorn and scoff at, and the INFJs often don't understand their intuition at a level which can be verbalized. Consequently, most INFJs are protective of their inner selves, sharing only what they choose to share when they choose to share it. They are deep, complex individuals,

Kermit the frog

who are quite private and typically difficult to understand. INFJs hold back part of themselves, and can be secretive. INFJs are sensitive, reserved, intense, creative, conceptual, concerned, compassionate individuals.

INFJs are complex, creative people with deep feelings and strong convictions that guide their lives. They are fascinated with original ways of looking at the world and are inspired by innovation and the chance to solve problems in creative ways. They are good at leading others toward positive changes with their gentle yet unswerving example. INFJs use their own inner vision to find meaning and new possibilities all around them.

"Shallow men believe in luck. Strong men believe in cause and effect.

Ralph Waldo Emerson

Often somewhat reserved, INFJs have a capacity for great warmth and empathy but are most comfortable sharing those feelings once they feel they know the person. They are thoughtful and careful decision makers, often needing plenty of time to reflect on issues in depth and consider the many implications before taking action. Bound by their convictions, INFJs are people of great integrity, willing to face resistance from others without backing down. They value harmony and cooperation and use praise and affirmation to motivate and win the loyalties of others.

An INFJs Career Choice Should Probably Include...

1. Using their intense inner vision, ability to establish harmonious relationships with others, and their skills in oral and written communication to obtain their goals.
2. Work that they believe in which allows them to use their imagination and creativity daily.
3. Working with abstraction, symbols, and imagination. great deal of technical, hands-on work or attention to details
4. The opportunity to work on a variety of issues, creating new programs, services, or solutions to challenging problems that help others.
5. A caring and supportive environment where their integrity is respected and where they are appreciated for their unique contributions.
6. Plenty of time to prepare and produce work they are proud of, organize their own time, and retain control and responsibility for their projects.

FAMOUS PEOPLE ~ INFJ PERSONALITY TYPE
Do you know what contributions these people provided to the world? If not, look up their names as discover their impact.

Sigmund Freud
Mother Teresa
J.R. Tolkien

John F. Kerry
Emily Dickinson
Ralph Waldo Emerson

INFP   Noble Provider of Aid to Society

Introvert, iNtuitive, Feeling, Perceiving - INFPs represent

Dewey in
Malcolm in the Middle

approximately 1% of the population. INFPs are highly intuitive about people. They are idealists and perfectionists, who drive themselves hard in their quest for achieving the goals they have identified for themselves. They rely heavily on their intuitions to guide them, and use their discoveries to constantly search for value in life. They are on a continuous mission to find the truth and meaning underlying things. Every encounter and every piece of knowledge gained gets sifted through the INFP's value system, and is evaluated to see if it has any potential to help the INFP define or refine their own path in life. The goal at the end of the path is always the same - the INFP is driven to help people and make the world a better place.

"No pessimist ever discovered the secret of the stars or sailed an uncharted land, or opened a new doorway for the human spirit.."

Helen Keller

Generally thoughtful and considerate, INFPs are good listeners and put people at ease. Although they may be reserved in expressing emotion, they have a very deep well of caring and are genuinely interested in understanding people. This sincerity is sensed by others, making the INFP a valued friend and confidante.

Harry Potter

An INFP can be quite warm with people he or she knows well. INFPs are adaptable, committed, compassionate, creative, loyal, and empathetic individuals.

INFPs are sensitive and idealistic people, who strive for inner harmony. Devoted to the people and things they care deeply about, they can be loyal and empathetic friends. While they appear cool and even detached, INFPs have private feelings which are strong and passionate. They trust their personal reactions and perceptions and use their own set of values to rule their lives.

"Man becomes great exactly in the degree in which he works for the welfare of his fellow-men."

Mohandas Ghandi

Doug Funnie

Curious about possibilities, INFPs enjoy all sorts of creative endeavors. Often insightful, they can be original thinkers who enjoy using their imagination to consider new ways of doing things. They can be very persuasive about their dreams and ideas, but only with people they trust, because they make such a personal investment in everything they do. Thoughtful and complex, INFPs are not especially interested in imposing their views on others but are very protective of their privacy and are highly selective about their friends.

An INFPs Career Choice Should Probably Include...

1. A position involved in working towards the public good, and in which they don't need to use hard logic.
2. The freedom to work on projects that inspire them, with plenty of time for quiet reflection.
3. Working with others who are committed to people-related values.

4. Working with people they trust and respect in a supportive and friendly environment.
5. The chance to consider and try creative approaches to problem solving that help other people improve their lives.
6. A cooperative environment with a minimum of bureaucracy.

FAMOUS PEOPLE ~ INFJ PERSONALITY TYPE
Do you know what contributions these people provided to the world? If not, look up their names as discover their impact.

Helen Keller   Shakespeare
Neil Diamond   Celine Dione
Mohandas Ghandi

| **INTJ** | **Mastermind Strategists** |

Stewie in *Family Guy*

Introvert, i**N**tuitive, **T**hinking, **J**udging – INTJ personalities represent approximately 1% of the population. INTJ's tremendous value and need for systems and organization, combined with their natural insightfulness, makes them excellent scientists. An INTJ scientist gives a gift to society by putting his/her ideas into a useful form for others to follow. It is not easy for the INTJ to express their internal images, insights, and abstractions. The internal form of the INTJ's thoughts and concepts is highly individualized, and is not readily translatable into a form that others will understand. However, the INTJ is driven to translate their ideas into a plan or system that is usually readily explainable, rather than to do a direct translation of their thoughts. They usually don't see the value of a direct transaction, and will also have difficulty expressing their ideas, which are nonlinear. However, their extreme respect of knowledge and intelligence will motivate them to explain themselves to another person who they feel is deserving of the effort.

"You simply have to put one foot in front of the other and keep going. Put blinders on and plow right ahead."

George Lucas

INTJs are natural leaders, although they usually choose to remain in the background until they see a real need to take over the lead. When they are in leadership roles, they are quite effective, because they are able to objectively see the reality of a situation, and are adaptable enough

Yoda in *Star Wars*

to change things which aren't working well. They are the supreme strategists - always scanning available ideas and concepts and weighing them against their current strategy, to plan for every conceivable contingency. INTJs are critical, autonomous, demanding, independent, logical, systems-oriented, and visionary individuals.

"I'm a great believer in luck, and I find the harder I work the more I have of it."

Thomas Jefferson

Lisa in
The Simpsons

INTJs have creative minds and an independent spirit. Logical and ingenious, they are confident in their ideas and their ability to meet or exceed their goals. They tend to aim high with everything they attempt and are driven to be competent and original in all they do. They have a keen sense of what is possible and have a global perspective. INTJs are good strategic thinkers, looking beyond what is known and seeing the inter-relatedness of elements.

Critical and demanding of themselves, with incredibly high standards, INTJs are not deterred or intimidated by opposition. They have great powers of concentration, and are so determined to see their vision become a reality, they will work with tireless energy to turn out a flawless idea or product.

An INTJs Career Choice Should Probably Include...

1. A position in academic, scientific, theoretical, or technical career that requires prolonged periods of solitary concentration and tough-minded analysis so their strengths in this area will be utilized.
2. The opportunity to work independently, thinking things though at great depth, and preparing fully before presenting their work.
3. Creative and intellectual challenges that keep them stimulated and involved with their work.
4. A position involved with planning, revising, or designing the future.
5. Evaluation and compensation that is based upon their perseverance and accomplishments, where they are respected by others in their field.
6. The freedom to take a task and run with it, maintain control over its outcome, and use their judgment and creativity to complete it according to their own high standards of success.

FAMOUS PEOPLE ~ INTJ PERSONALITY TYPE
Do you know what contributions these people provided to the world? If not, look up their names as discover their impact.

C.S. Lewis   Friedrich Nietzsche
Thomas Jefferson   Sally Jesse Rafael
George Lucas   Dwight Eisenhower
Alan Greenspan   Phil Jackson

INTP   **Troubleshooters of the world**

Dr. Emmett Brown in
Back to the Future

Introvert, iNtuitive, Thinking, Perceiving – INTP personalities represent approximately 1% of the population. INTPs value knowledge above all else. Their minds are constantly working to generate new theories, or to prove or disprove existing theories. They approach problems and theories with enthusiasm and skepticism, ignoring existing rules and opinions and defining their own approach to the resolution. They seek patterns and logical explanations for anything that interests them. They're usually extremely bright, and able to be objectively critical in their analysis. They love new ideas, and become very excited over abstractions and theories. They love to discuss these concepts with others. They may seem "dreamy" and distant to others, because they spend a lot of time inside their minds musing over theories. They hate to work on routine things - they would much prefer to build complex theoretical solutions, and leave the implementation of the system to others. They are intensely interested in theory, and will put forth tremendous amounts of time and energy into finding a solution to a problem with has piqued their interest.

"Imagination is more important than knowledge... "

Albert Einstein

INTPs do not like to lead or control people. They're very tolerant and flexible in most situations, unless one of their firmly held beliefs has been violated or challenged, in which case they may take a very rigid stance. The INTP is likely to be very shy when it comes to meeting new people. On the other hand, the INTP is very self-confident and

Dexter in *Dexter's Laboratory*

gregarious around people they know well, or when discussing theories which they fully understand. INTPs are autonomous, curious, detached, inquisitive, logical, original, skeptical, and theoretical individuals.

INTPs are great strategic thinkers and creative problem solvers. They are especially interested in mastering and perfecting theoretical or complex issues. Quiet, serious, and thoughtful, INTPs are usually intellectual and complicated people who appear quite dispassionate and reserved. However, they can become excited and persuasive about their ideas once they are ready to share them. INTPs are logical and analytical people, with a strong need to make sense of things.

> *"I have been impressed with the urgency of doing. Knowing is not enough; we must apply. Being willing is not enough; we must do."*
>
> Leonardo da Vinci

Strongly independent, INTPs are driven to increase their personal mastery of subjects and are drawn to people of power and expertise. They tend to be open minded, intrigued with anything imaginative, and may enjoy risk taking. They prefer to look beyond what is known or accepted at the present time and consider more creative yet reasonable approaches to problems or ways of perfecting systems.

An INTPs Career Choice Should Probably Include...

1. Working in-depth on one creative challenge at a time and the opportunity to give it their full attention without a lot of interruptions.
2. The chance to apply logic to theories to find solutions and develop innovative approaches and systems but not get bogged down in the details of implementation.
3. Work that has very high standards for performance, matching their own high standards.
4. An atmosphere of professionalism and mutual respect, where their expertise is recognized and respected and

they have some say in how they are evaluated and compensated.
5. The chance to logically analyze existing and potential systems and make recommendations for strategically sound changes.
6. An unstructured environment that encourages free thinking and improvisation, without senseless rules, unnecessary meetings, or paperwork.

FAMOUS PEOPLE ~ INTP PERSONALITY TYPE
Do you know what contributions these people provided to the world? If not, look up their names as discover their impact.

Abraham Lincoln   Albert Einstein
Michael Moore   Kurt Cobaine
Stephen King   Leonardo da Vinci

ISFJ   The Protector

Introvert, Sensing, Feeling, Judging – ISFJ personalities represent approximately 6% of the population. ISFJs are warm, kindhearted individuals who want to believe the best of people and they bring an aura of quiet warmth, caring, and dependability to all that they do. They live in a concrete world and value harmony and cooperation, and are likely to be very sensitive to other people's feelings. People value the ISFJ for their consideration and awareness, and their ability to bring out the best in others by their firm desire to believe the best.

Marge in *The Simpsons*

"It's not necessary to fear the prospect of failure but to be determined not to fail. "

Jimmy Carter

ISFJs have a rich inner world not usually obvious to observers. They constantly take in information about people and situations that is personally important to them, and store it away. This tremendous store of information is usually startlingly accurate, because the ISFJ has an exceptional memory about things that are important to their value systems. It would not be uncommon for the ISFJ to remember a particular facial expression or conversation in precise detail years after the event occurred, if the situation made an impression on them. ISFJs are conscientious, conservative, patient, practical, meticulous, service-minded and loyal individuals.

Charlie in *Charlie and the Chocolate Factory*

ISFJs are hard working and conscientious individuals prone to be quiet and serious. They tend to be realistic and down to earth and exhibit great patience for detail. They have good memories for facts and details and are painstakingly accurate. They have good common sense and tend to make conservative, thoughtful, and sensible decisions, but they want, and need, clear directions and explicit expectations.

"I want to live my life, not record it."

Jacquelyn Kennedy Onassis

ISFJs are caring people interested in the concerns and feelings of others. They are quiet and modest people who prefer to share their feelings and deep convictions only with those they know well. They are protective, loyal, and devoted friends and take great pride and satisfaction from the accomplishments of their friends and family. ISFJs have a strong work ethic working hard, doing whatever is needed until the job is finished.

An ISFJs Career Choice Should Probably Include...

1. The opportunity to work steadily on one project at a time, without a lot of interruptions or changes in plan.
2. Work that requires accuracy and attention to detail, organization, and adherence to standard operating procedures.
3. Work that lets them use a personal approach to helping others, preferably on a one-on-one basis.
4. An environment that is structured and stable, where they know what is expected of them and they are rewarded for their hard work and contribution.
5. Work that is of a practical nature and is service-oriented, so they can see that they are helping others in real and tangible ways.

FAMOUS PEOPLE ~ ISFJ PERSONALITY TYPE
Do you know what contributions these people provided to the world? If not, look up their names as discover their impact.

Jimmy Carter   Laura Bush
Kristi Yamaguchi   Jacquelyn Kennedy Onassis

ISFP   The Composer

Introvert, Sensing, Feeling, Perceiving – ISFP personalities represent approximately 6% of the population. ISFPs live in the world of sensation and possibilities and are in tune with the way things look, taste, sound, feel, and smell. They have a strong aesthetic appreciation for art, and are likely to be artists in some form, because they are unusually gifted at creating and composing things which will strongly affect the senses. They have a strong set of values, which they strive to

Velma from
Scooby Doo

consistently meet in their lives. They need to feel as if they're living their lives in accordance with what they feel is right, and will rebel against anything which conflicts with that goal. They're likely to choose jobs and careers which allow them the freedom of working towards the realization of their value-oriented personal goals.

ISFPs tend to be quiet and reserved, and difficult to get to know well. They hold back their ideas and opinions except from those who they are closest to. They are likely to be kind, gentle and sensitive in their dealings with others. They are interested in contributing to people's sense of well-being and happiness, and will put a great deal of effort and energy into tasks which they believe in. ISFPs are caring, flexible, empathetic, harmonious, spontaneous, and trusting individuals.

ISFPs are gentle, soft-spoken, and modest people. On the surface, they often appear cool and impassive but really have deep and passionate feelings that they share only with people they know well and trust. They are loyal, devoted, and patient friends, not particularly interested in trying to control or impose their values on others. They are trusting and sensitive, and need their personal and professional relationships to be harmonious and tension free.

Chris Griffin in
Family Guy

Realistic, sensible, and down to earth, ISFPs are concerned with enjoying life and experiencing all things to the fullest. ISFPs have a spontaneous and playful disposition and tend to respond to events rather than plan ahead. Often artistic, ISFPs notice the beauty in everything around them and enjoy spending their free time on their hobbies or crafts. They tend to have a small, tight knit group of friends and strive to maintain a balance in their lives, not placing work above the other things that matter most to them. They are quick-witted and spatial in their thinking identifying opportunities of a situation and quickly acting to take advantage of them.

An ISFPs Career Choice Should Probably Include...

1. A career which is more than just a job to them and is consistent with their strong core of inner values.
2. An affirming, supportive, and noncompetitive atmosphere without a lot of hidden political agendas.
3. Work that has a real and practical purpose where they can see and experience how they are able to help other people.
4. A balance between working alone and working one-on-one, where the pace of their work is within their control.
5. An opportunity to exhibit their original and unconventional abilities.
6. The opportunity to work on a variety of projects that they believe in and where each day is different from the one before.

FAMOUS PEOPLE ~ ISFP PERSONALITY TYPE
Do you know what contributions these people provided to the world? If not, look up their names as discover their impact.

Bob Marley   Picasso
Michael Jackson   Paul McCartney
Mozart   Andre 3000 *from Outkast*

ISTJ   The Duty Seekers

Introvert, Sensing, Thinking, Judging - ISTJs represent approximately 6% of the population. ISTJs are quiet and reserved individuals who are interested in security and peaceful living. They are loyal, faithful, conservative, decisive, factual, organized, realistic, sensible, and dependable

Shrek

individuals. ISTJs are quiet, serious, and traditional people, who communicate in a style that is clear, simple, and direct. They are careful observers with a realistic and practical perspective that guides their lives. They notice details that interest or relate to them and have great memories for thing they have personally experienced. They like to think things through before acting and tend to be cautious about change. ISTJs are responsible, stable, and capable in all situations they know.

Conscientious and logical, ISTJs like to make decisions that are sensible and that help things stay orderly arid efficient. Very organized and productive, they are duty bound, hard workers with a great ability to concentrate and get things done. They like to be judged on their merits and are fair and consistent when dealing with others. They take all their commitments seriously and prefer people who are genuine and down to earth. They have a strong internal sense of duty which lends them a serious air and the motivation to follow through on tasks and they are extremely dependable on following through with things which they have promised. Organized and methodical in their approach, they can generally succeed at any task which they undertake. They place great importance on honesty and integrity and can be depended on to do the right thing for their families and communities.

Simon in *Alvin and the Chipmunks*

While they generally take things very seriously, ISTJs also usually have an offbeat sense of humor and can be a lot of fun - especially at family or work-related gatherings. They tend to believe in laws and traditions, and expect the same from others. They're not comfortable with breaking laws or going against the rules. If they are able to see a good reason for stepping outside of the established mode of doing things, the ISTJ will support that effort. However, ISTJs more often tend to believe that things should be done according to procedures and plans, almost to a fault. If taken too far, the need for procedure and plans may become an obsession with structure, leading them to do everything "by the book." ISTJs have a strong sense of duty and they sometimes get more work piled on them than they can reasonably handle because their sense of duty makes it difficult for them to say "No."

An ISTJs Career Choice Should Probably Include...

1. The opportunity to use their excellent organizational skills and their powers of concentration to create order and structure.
2. A position in which precision and technological know-how are required and they can work with facts and concrete information
3. A stable and traditional work environment, with a clear reporting structure and explicit expectations.
4. The opportunity to work on one project at a time, with plenty of time to plan their work and execute it without interruption.
5. Work that involves real products and services, where they can see the immediate results of their efforts, and where they are evaluated on their merits.
6. A promotional system that rewards their hard work, experience, and accomplishments with increasing levels of responsibility and compensation.

FAMOUS PEOPLE ~ ISTJ PERSONALITY TYPE
Do you know what contributions these people provided to the world? If not, look up their names as discover their impact.

George Bush
Dick Cheney
Cal Ripken, Jr.

Harry Truman
Pete Sampras

ISTP   Ready to Try it Once Adventurer

Abigail "Abby" Lincoln
aka Nubumuh Five in
Kids Next Door

Introvert, Sensing, Thinking, Perceiving - ISTPs represent approximately 6% of the population. ISTPs are good at logical analysis and like to use it on practical concerns. They typically have strong powers of reasoning, although they're not interested in theories or concepts unless they can see a practical application. They like to take things apart and see how they work. ISTPs have an adventuresome spirit and they are attracted to motorcycles, airplanes, sky diving, surfing, etc. They thrive on action and are usually fearless. ISTPs are fiercely independent, needing to have the space to make their own decisions about their next step. They do not believe in or follow rules and regulations, as this would prohibit their ability to "do their own thing." Their sense of adventure and desire for constant action makes ISTPs prone to becoming bored rather quickly.

ISTPs are action-oriented people. They like to be up and about, doing things. They are not people to sit behind a desk all day and do long-range planning. Adaptable and spontaneous, they respond to what is immediately before them. They usually have strong technical skills, and can be effective technical leaders. They focus on details and practical things. They have an excellent sense of expediency and grasp of the details which enables them to make quick, effective decisions.

ISTPs are generally quiet and independent people who like, and need, to spend time alone because this is when they can sort things out in their minds most clearly. They like to be busy and involved with projects that are of importance and interest to them and they value skills and quality performance in themselves and others. Rather reserved and private, ISTPs do not usually share their reactions or responses unless urged to do so. They tend to be straightforward, honest, and more interested in action than conversation, unless it is a subject about which they know a lot. Unpretentious and down to earth, ISTPs operate more on curiosity and impulses than organization or plans.

ISTPs usually have a good sense of how mechanical things work and are logical in their analysis. They are realistic in their assessments and trust hard facts they have gained through personal experience. They are good observers and enjoy working with real things. ISTPs tend to be spontaneous and easy going, always ready and eager to get involved with fun or physical activities, especially those out-of-doors or containing a level of risk, thrill, or excitement.

An ISTPs Career Choice Should Probably Include...

1. A profession requiring a tough-minded, analytical, and realistic approach to its work.
2. Work that is clearly defined and specific in nature, where they master and then use their well-developed logical skills.
3. The opportunity to work at their own pace, independently, without a lot of restrictions on their activities or demands on their time.
4. An environment that is relaxed and informal, where they work along side other skilled people they respect and who respect them.
5. Work involving a craftsman-like approach in which they can utilize their skills in working with tools or instruments.
6. The opportunity to engage in short-term problem solving, troubleshooting activities, and crisis management.

FAMOUS PEOPLE ~ ISTP PERSONALITY TYPE

50-Cent	Eminem
Michael Jordan	Ozzy Osbourne
Clint Eastwood	Lance Armstrong

CHAPTER 8   JETSON AGE CAREER OPTIONS

As the recession continues and technology changes rapidly, many jobs become obsolete and others become high demand.

What are the high demand jobs of the future?

The place to find detailed information is the Bureau of Labor Statistics (BLS). It provides all sorts of information regarding careers salaries and need for careers.

FASTEST GROWING OCCUPATION

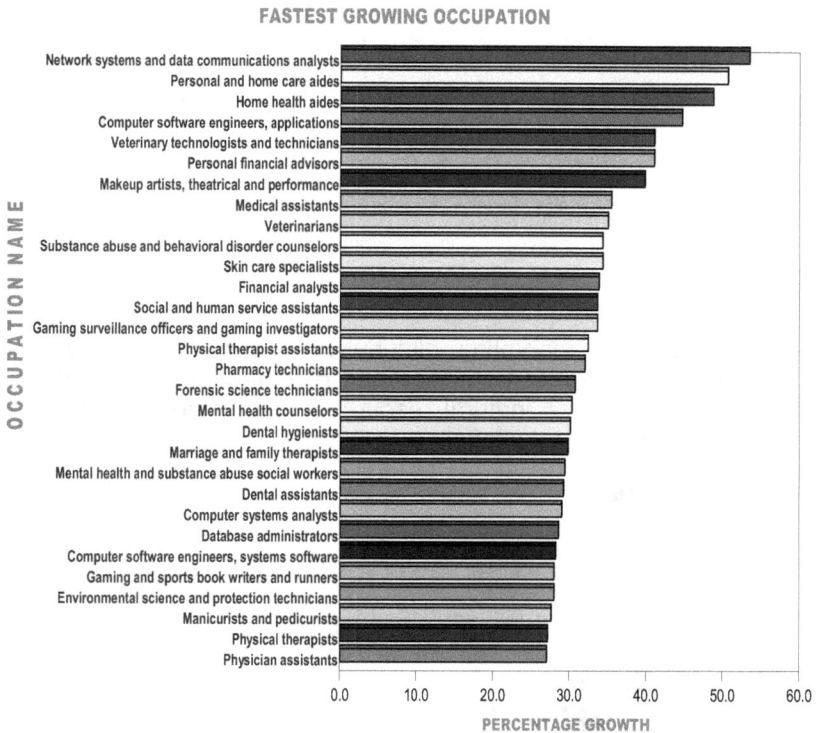

OCCUPATION NAME

- Network systems and data communications analysts
- Personal and home care aides
- Home health aides
- Computer software engineers, applications
- Veterinary technologists and technicians
- Personal financial advisors
- Makeup artists, theatrical and performance
- Medical assistants
- Veterinarians
- Substance abuse and behavioral disorder counselors
- Skin care specialists
- Financial analysts
- Social and human service assistants
- Gaming surveillance officers and gaming investigators
- Physical therapist assistants
- Pharmacy technicians
- Forensic science technicians
- Mental health counselors
- Dental hygienists
- Marriage and family therapists
- Mental health and substance abuse social workers
- Dental assistants
- Computer systems analysts
- Database administrators
- Computer software engineers, systems software
- Gaming and sports book writers and runners
- Environmental science and protection technicians
- Manicurists and pedicurists
- Physical therapists
- Physician assistants

PERCENTAGE GROWTH

0.0   10.0   20.0   30.0   40.0   50.0   60.0

Here are the fastest growing careers/ occupations based on percentages through 2016 as reported by the Bureau of Labor Statistics (BLS). Notice the areas where the projected growth percentage seem to be the highest. Are there any themes that seem to jump out at you? It appears technology is the driver of growth and most of the jobs to be created center around technology and creativity

There are 16 Career Clusters as defined by the Federal Government. Icons reprinted with permission of disclosure. Here are the Top 50 High Demand Occupations earning above $20 per hour based on the number of jobs to be created. [35] To determine what the annual salary is multiply the Hourly Wage by 2080 hours. This is the salary for a typical 40 hour work week.

Career Clusters and Fastest Growing Careers

Agriculture, Food & Natural Resources

The production, processing, marketing, distribution, financing, and development of agricultural commodities and resources including food, fiber, wood products, natural resources, horticulture, and other plant and animal products/resources.

Architecture & Construction

Architecture and Construction careers are responsible for designing, planning, managing, building and maintaining the built environment.

Occupation Title	Projected Need for Employees (2006 - 2016)	Projected Growth	2006 Median Hourly Wage Range[2]	Education & Training Required[3]
Construction Managers	152,000	9-17%	$37	29% College Degree
Electricians	234,000	0-8%	$22	7% College Degree
Construction Trades and Extraction Managers	178,000	9-17%	$27	10% College Degree
Mechanics, Installers, and Repairers Managers	143,000	0-8%	$27	13% College Degree
Plumbers, Pipefitters, and Steamfitters	157,000	9-17%	$21	3% College Degree
Cost Estimators	86,000	18-26%	$26	32% College Degree

Arts, A/V Technology & Communications

Designing, producing, exhibiting, performing, writing, and publishing multimedia content including visual and performing arts and design, journalism, and entertainment services.

iness Management & Administration

Business Management and Administration careers encompass planning, organizing, directing and evaluating business functions essential to efficient and productive business operations. Business Management and Administration career opportunities are available in every sector of the economy.

Occupation Title	Projected Need for Employees (2006 - 2016)	Projected Growth	2006 Median Hourly Wage Range[2]	Education & Training Required[3]
General and Operations Managers	441,000	0-8%	$43	47% College Degree
Accountants and Auditors	450,000	18-26%	$27	79% College Degree
Management Analysts	264,000	18-26%	$34	77% College Degree
Chief Executives	118,000	0-8%	$70+	65% College Degree
Office and Administrative Support Managers	374,000	0-8%	$21	29% College Degree
Administrative Services Managers	94,000	9-17%	$34	40% College Degree

Planning, managing and providing education and training services, and related learning support services.

Occupation Title	Projected Need for Employees (2006 - 2016)	Projected Growth	2006 Median Hourly Wage Range[2]	Education & Training Required[3]
Elementary School Teachers	545,000	3-17%	$23	95% College Degree
Secondary School Teachers	368,000	0-8%	$24	95% College Degree
Middle School Teachers	217,000	3-17%	$23	95% College Degree
Teacher Assistants	350,000	0-17%	$10	18% College Degree
Education Administrators, K-12	80,000	0-8%	$39	78% College Degree
Special Education Teachers, K-6	92,000	18-26%	$23	87% College Degree

Planning, services for financial and investment planning, banking, insurance, and business financial management.

Occupation Title	Projected Need for Employees (2006 - 2016)	Projected Growth	2006 Median Hourly Wage Range[2]	Education & Training Required[3]
Securities, Commodities, and Financial Services Sales Agents	161,000	18-26%	$33	67% College Degree
Insurance Sales Agents	151,000	9-17%	$21	45% College Degree
Financial Managers	138,000	9-17%	$46	60% College Degree
Financial Analysts	87,000	27+%	$34	87% College Degree
Personal Financial Advisors	88,000	27+%	$33	81% College Degree
Claims Adjusters, Examiners, and Investigators	105,000	9-17%	$26	47% College Degree

overnment & Public Administration

Executing governmental functions to include Governance; National Security; Foreign Service; Planning; Revenue and Taxation; Regulation; and Management and Administration at the local, state, and federal levels.

Health Science

Planning, managing, and providing therapeutic services, diagnostic services, health informatics, support services, and biotechnology research and development.

Occupation Title	Projected Need for Employees (2006 - 2016)	Projected Growth	2006 Median Hourly Wage Range[2]	Education & Training Required[3]
Registered Nurses	1,001,000	18-26%	$29	56% College Degree
Physicians and Surgeons	204,000	9-17%	$70+	100% College Degree
Pharmacists	95,000	18-26%	$48	97% College Degree
Medical and Health Services Managers	92,000	9-17%	$37	57% College Degree
Dentists, General	39,000	9-17%	$66	100% College Degree
Dental Hygienists	82,000	27+%	$31	33% College Degree
Physical Therapists	68,000	27+%	$34	89% College Degree

Hospitality & Tourism encompasses the management, marketing and operations of restaurants and other foodservices, lodging, attractions, recreation events and travel related services.

Preparing individuals for employment in career pathways that relate to families and human needs.

Building Linkages in IT Occupations Framework: For Entry Level, Technical, and Professional Careers Related to the Design, Development, Support and Management of Hardware, Software, Multimedia, and Systems Integration Services.

Occupation Title	Projected Need for Employees (2006 - 2016)	Projected Growth	2006 Median Hourly Wage Range[2]	Education & Training Required[3]
Computer Systems Analysts	280,000	27+%	$35	68% College Degree

Network Systems and Data Communications Analysts	193,000	27+%	$33	57% College Degree
Computer Support Specialists	242,000	9-17%	$20	43% College Degree
Network and Computer Systems Administrators	154,000	27+%	$31	50% College Degree
Computer and Information Systems Managers	86,000	9-17%	$52	50% College Degree

Public Safety, Corrections & Security Planning, managing, and providing legal, public safety, protective services and homeland security, including professional and technical support services.

Occupation Title	Projected Need for Employees (2006 - 2016)	Projected Growth	2006 Median Hourly Wage Range[2]	Education & Training Required[3]
Lawyers	228,000	9-17%	$51	99% College Degree
Police and Sheriff's Patrol Officers	243,000	9-17%	$24	32% College Degree
Fire Fighters	142,000	9-17%	$21	18% College Degree

Manufacturing is planning, managing and performing the processing of materials into intermediate or final products and related professional and technical support activities such as production planning and control, maintenance and manufacturing/process engineering.

Occupation Title	Projected Need for Employees (2006 - 2016)	Projected Growth	2006 Median Hourly Wage Range[2]	Education & Training Required[3]
Sales Representatives, Wholesale and Manufacturing,	476,000	0-8%	$24	51% College Degree

Marketing Planning, managing, and performing marketing activities to reach organizational objectives.

Occupation Title	Projected Need for Employees (2006 - 2016)	Projected Growth	2006 Median Hourly Wage Range[2]	Education & Training Required[3]
Sales Managers	103,000	9-17%	$46	69% College Degree

Sales Representatives, Technical and Scientific Products	142,000	 0-17%	$33	51% College Degree
Marketing Managers	61,000	 9-17%	$50	69% College Degree
Real Estate Sales Agents	115,000	 9-17%	$20	45% College Degree

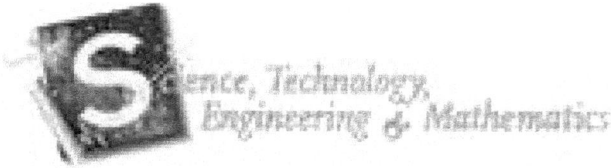

is planning, managing, and providing scientific research and professional and technical services (e.g., physical science, social science, engineering) including laboratory and testing services, and research and development services.

Occupation Title	Projected Need for Employees (2006 - 2016)	Projected Growth	2006 Median Hourly Wage Range[2]	Education & Training Required[3]
Computer Software Engineers, Applications	300,000	 27+%	$40	85% College Degree
Computer Software Engineers, Systems Software	150,000	 27+%	$43	85% College Degree

Civil Engineers	114,000	18-26%	$34	87% College Degree
Industrial Engineers	89,000	18-26%	$34	73% College Degree
Engineering Managers	51,000	0-8%	$53	84% College Degree

ransportation, Distribution & Logistics

Planning, management, and movement of people, materials, and goods by road, pipeline, air, rail and water and related professional and technical support services such as transportation infrastructure planning and management, logistics services, mobile equipment and facility maintenance.

Occupation Title	Projected Need for Employees (2006 - 2016)	Projected Growth	2006 Median Hourly Wage Range[2]	Education & Training Required[3]
Airline Pilots, Copilots, and Flight Engineers	33,000	9-17%	$68	73% College Degree

Careers By Personality Type

Here are careers that fit your personality type.[36] There is a career highlight followed by careers suitable for your personality type. Go to www.escapetocollege.com and play **Drive of Your Life** game. Register. Research at least 20 careers in your personality type there. Since it is a game the more careers you research the higher your total score will be. GO FOR IT!

ENFJ Career Highlight

Urban Planner

Planners make new plans when more people move into a community. They might tell community leaders that they need new schools or roads. Before making plans for a community, planners need to know where everything is. They find out how many people use the streets, highways, water, sewers, schools, libraries, museums, and parks.

Education
Bachelor's or Master in Urban Design/ Urban Planning

Salary/ Wage
Median Annual Income	$57,935
Median Hourly Income	$27.85

ENFJ (Extraverted, Intuitive, Feeling, Judging) Careers

Adult day care coordinator	Advertising account executive
Bilingual education teacher	Career counselor
Child Life Specialist	Child welfare worker
Chiropractor	Clergy/minister
Coach	College or university administrator
College professor (humanities)	Communications director
Composer	Content editor for Web site
Copy writer	Corporate outplacement counselor
Corporate/team trainer	Counselor
Customer relations manager	Dental hygienist
Desktop publishing specialist	Dietitian/nutritionist
Diplomat	Director of assisted care facility

Director of child care facility
Educational program director
Entertainer/artist
Executive (small business)
Graphic artist
Holistic health practitioner
Human resource trainer
Interpreter/translator
Librarian
Marketing executive (broadcast)
Multimedia producer
Newscaster
Occupational therapist
Outplacement consultant
Personnel recruiter
Planned-giving officer
Probation officer
Psychologist
Public relations specialist
Reporter and correspondent
Set designer
Social scientist
Sociologist

Editor
Educational psychologist
Event planner
Fund-raiser
Guidance counselor
Hotel and restaurant manager
Human resources recruiter
Labor relations manager
Management consultant
Marketing manager
Music director
Nonprofit organization director
Optometrist
Instructor, Parent development
Philanthropic consultant
Politician
Project manager
Public health educator
Recreational director
Sales manager/trainer
Social service director
Social worker
Special education teacher

Speech-language pathologist/audiologist
Teacher (health, art, drama, English)
Therapist
Travel agent
Urban and regional planner

Technology advocate
TV producer
Writer/journalist

ENFP Career Highlight

Advertising Account Executive

Advertising Account Executives manage the account services department, assesses the need for advertising and, in advertising agencies, maintains the accounts of clients.

Education
Bachelor's or Master in Business /Marketing

Salary/ Wage
Median Annual Income	$73,060
Median Hourly Income	$35.13

ENFP (Extraverted, Intuitive, Feeling, Perceiving) Careers

Advertising account manager/executive
Advertising creative director
Artist
Broadcast news analyst
Cartoonist or animator
Chemist
Child welfare counselor
Coach
Computer programmer/specialist
Consultant
Corrections officer
Counseling psychologist
Desktop publisher
Documentary filmmaker
Editor/art director (Web sites)
Educational psychologist
Entrepreneur
Event planner
Exhibit designer
Holistic health practitioner
Information-graphics designer
Interior designer
Labor relations manager
Librarian
Medical assistant
Multimedia producer
Newscaster
Ombudsperson
Personnel recruiter
Physical therapist
Politician
Public relations specialist
Rehabilitation worker
Reporter/editor/art director (magazine)
Research assistant
Restaurateur
Sales (intangibles/ideas)
Social scientist
Special education teacher
Speech-language pathologist/audiologist
Strategic planner

Anthropologist
Bilingual education teacher
Career counselor
Character actor
Child Life Specialist
Chiropractor
Columnist
Computer systems analyst
Corporate/team trainer
Costume and wardrobe designer
Customer relations manager
Dietitian/nutritionist
Early childhood education teacher
Education software developer
Employee assistance counselor
Environmental attorney
Executive (Radio, TV, cable)
High school guidance counselor
Human resources manager/trainer
Insurance agent
Inventor
Legal mediator
Marketing consultant
Merchandise planner
Musician/composer
Occupational therapist
Instructor, child development
Philanthropic consultant
Planned-giving officer
Public health educator
Publicist
Religious/pastoral counselor
Residential housing director
Screenwriter/playwright
Social psychologist
Social worker
Technology consultant

Teacher (humanities)   Television producer
Theater director   Travel agent
Urban regional planner

ENTJ Career Highlight

Environmental Engineer

Environmental engineers develop solutions to environmental problems using the principles of biology and chemistry. They study and attempt to minimize the effects of acid rain, global warming, automobile emissions, ozone depletion and hazardous waste.

Education
Bachelor's or Master in Engineering

Salary/ Wage

Median Annual Income	$69,940
Median Hourly Income	$33.63

ENTJ (Extraverted, Intuitive, Thinking, Judging) Careers

Accountant   Actor
Advertising account manager   Architect
Biologist   Business consultant
Chemical engineer   Chief executive officer
College/university administrator   Computer/information consultant
Corporate finance attorney   Corporate team trainer
Database manager   Dentist
Economic analyst   Economist
Educational consultant
Employment development specialist
Environmental engineer   Executive (Radio, TV, cable)
Fine artist   Franchise owner
Human resources manager   Information services sales
International banker   International sales and marketing
Investment banker   Journalist
Judge   Labor relations manager
Lawyer   Legislative assistant

Life scientist
Local Area Network (LAN) administrator

Logistics consultant — Management trainer
Marketing manager — Media planner/buyer
Minister/clergy — Mortgage broker
Network administrator — Network integration specialist
Office manager — Pathologist
Personal financial planner — Personnel manager
Photographer — Physician
Pilot — Police and detective supervisor
Political consultant — Political scientist
Program designer — Psychiatrist
Psychologist — Real estate manager
Retail manager — Robotics network manager
Sales manager — School principal
Stockbroker — Systems administrator

Teacher (English, science, social studies)
Telecommunications security consultant
Theater producer
Treasurer, controller, chief financial officer
Venture capitalist

ENTP Career Highlight

Financial Planner

Financial planners use their knowledge of investments, tax laws, and insurance to recommend financial options to individuals. Planners help clients with retirement and estate planning, funding the college education of children, and general investment choices.

Education
Bachelor's or Master preferably in Finance, Economics

Salary/ Wage
Median Annual Income	$66,120
Median Hourly Income	$31.79

ENTP (Extraverted, Intuitive, Thinking, Perceiving) Careers

Actor

Advertising creative director

Aeronautical engineer

Art director (magazine)

Athletic coach or scout

Attorney (litigator)

Broadcast news analyst

Business manager

Chiropractor

Columnist, critic, or commentator

Computer analyst

Computer programmer

Computer specialist

Computer systems analyst

Copy writer

Corrections officer

Creative director/multimedia

Creative writer

Credit investigator

Criminalist/ ballistics expert

Desktop publisher/specialist

Detective

Director—stage or motion pictures

Diversity manager/trainer

Educational psychologist

Employee relations specialist

Engineer

Entrepreneur

Environmental scientist

Event planner

Financial planner

Foreign language teacher

Home economist

Hotel/motel manager

Human resources recruiter

Industrial design manager

Informational-graphics designer

International marketing

Internet architect

Internet marketer

Inventor

Investment banker/broker

Journalist

Lawyer

Literary agent

Logistics consultant—

Management consultant

Marketing researcher/planner

Motivational speaker

Network integration specialist

New business developer—information services

Ombudsperson

Optometrist

Outplacement consultant

Personnel systems developer

Photographer

Political analyst

Political manager

Politician

Producer

Property manager

Psychologist

Public relations specialist

Radio/TV talk show host

Real estate agent/developer

Reporter or correspondent

Restaurant/bar owner

Sales Securities/commodities

Security analyst

Social scientist

Speech pathologist

Sports marketer

Strategic planner

Student personnel administrator

Technical trainer

University or college president

Urban/regional planner

Venture capitalist

ESFJ Career Highlight

Legislative Assistant

Legislative assistants provide technical assistance in the legal field including researching law, investigating facts, and examining public records. Assist legislators in developing laws and statutes for the federal, state and local levels.

Education
High School Diploma and/or 1-2 years training

Salary/ Wage

Median Annual Income	$38,190
Median Hourly Income	$18.36

ESFJ (Extraverted, Sensing, Feeling, Judging) Careers

Accountant	Actor
Aerobics instructor	Athletic coach
Bilingual education teacher	Bookkeeper
Caterer	Chemist
Child care center director	Child life specialist
Child provider	Child welfare counselor
Chiropractor	Clergy—minister/priest/rabbi
Community welfare worker	Corrective therapist
Cosmetologist/hairdresser	Counselor
Court clerk	Court reporter
Credit counselor	
Customer relations manager (technology)	
Customer service manager/representative	
Dentist/dental hygienist	Dialysis technician
Dietitian/nutritionist	Director of religious education
Eco-tourism specialist	Employee assistance counselor
Executive (Radio, TV, cable)	Exercise physiologist
Family physician	Flight attendant
Food service manager	Fund-raiser
Funeral home director	Genealogist
Health care administrator	Health club manager

Home health social worker/aide
Hotel/motel manager
Land leasing and development specialist
Law clerk
Licensed practical nurse (LPN)
Lodging owner/innkeeper
Medical secretary
Merchandise planner
Nursery and greenhouse manager
Office manager
Paralegal or legal assistant
Personal fitness trainer
Physical therapist
Primary care physician
Psychologist
Public relations accountant executive
Public relations specialist
Real estate agent/broker/appraise
Respiratory therapist
Sales representative (tangibles)
Secretary
Speech pathologist
Sports equipment/merchandise sales
Student personnel administrator
Teacher (elementary, secondary, special education)
Translator/interpreter
Typist
Wilderness adventure leader

Hospice worker
Insurance agent

Legislative assistant
Loan officer and counselor
Management consultant
Medical/dental assistant
Nurse
Nursing instructor
Optometrist/optician
Personal banker
Pharmacist/pharmacy technician
Police detective
Property manager

Radiological technician
Recreational therapist
Retail owner/operator
School principal
Social worker

Substance abuse counselor

Travel agent
Veterinarian

ESFJ Career Highlight

Pharmacy Technicians

Pharmacy technicians help licensed Pharmacists provide medication and other health care products to patients. Technicians usually perform routine tasks to help prepare prescribed medication, such as counting tablets and labeling bottles.

Education
High School Diploma and/or 1-2 years formal training

Salary/ Wage

Median Annual Income	$25,626
Median Hourly Income	$12.32

ESFP (Extraverted, Sensing, Feeling, Perceiving) Careers

Aerobics instructor
Athletic coach
Cartoonist and animator
Chef or head cook
Child life specialist
Costume/wardrobe specialist
Dietitian/nutritionist
Education software developer
Environmental scientist
Film producer
Fund-raiser
Home care worker/health aide
Human resources diversity manager
Insurance agent/broker (health, life)
Insurance fraud investigator
Labor relations mediator
Landscape architect
Marine biologist
Musician
Nurse/nursing instructor
Optician/Optometrist
Park naturalist
Performer (dancer, comedian)
Pharmacy technician
Physician
Police/corrections officer
Psychologist
Radio/television announcer
Real estate agent
Recreational therapist
Retail sales/management
Social conservationist
Social worker
Speech and language pathologist
Teacher
Transplant coordinator
Travel sales/broker
Vocational rehabilitation counselor
Zoologist

Art therapist
Cardiology technologist
Character actor
Child care provider
Chiropractor
Dental assistant and hygienist
Dog trainer
Entertainment and sports agent
Exercise physiologist
Floral designer
Geologist
Hospice worker

Interior designer
Landscape and grounds manager
Medical technician
Merchandise displayer/planner
News anchor
Occupational therapist
Painter/illustrator/sculptor
Pediatrician
Personal fitness trainer
Photographer
Podiatrist
Promoter
Public relations specialist
Radiological technician
Receptionist
Respiratory therapist
Secretary
Social scientist
Special events coordinator
Substance abuse counselor
Team trainer
Travel agent/tour operator
Veterinarian/veterinary assistant

ESTJ Career Highlight

Insurance adjuster

Adjusters plan and schedule the work required to process a claim. They investigate claims by interviewing the claimant and witnesses, consulting police and hospital records, and inspecting property damage to determine the extent of the company's liability.

Education
High School Diploma and/or 1-2 years training

Salary/ Wage

Median Annual Income	$50,660
Median Hourly Income	$24.36

ESTJ (Extroverted, Sensing, Thinking, Judging) Careers

Accounting internal auditor	Administrator
Athletic coach	Athletic trainer
Auditor	Aviation inspector
Bank manager/loan officer	Budget analyst
Chief information officer	
Civil/mechanical/metallurgical engineer	
Clergy/minister	Clinical technician
Commercial airplane pilot	Community health worker
Computer analyst	Cook
Corporate finance lawyer	Court clerk
Credit analyst/counselor	Database administrator/manager
Dentist	EEG technician
Environmental inspector	Executive
Factory supervisor	Funeral director
General contractor	Government employee
Hospitality manager	Industrial engineer
Insurance adjuster	Insurance agent
Judge	Lawyer
Legislative assistant	Licensing examiner/inspector
Logistics and supply manager	Management consultant
Network administrator	Office manager

Paralegal
Pharmaceutical sales
Physician, general medicine
Police/probations/corrections officer
Primary care physician
Project manager
Public relations specialist
Real estate agent/appraiser
Regulatory compliance officer
Sales Securities/commodities
School principal
Social services worker
Sports merchandiser
Teacher, technical trades
Telecommunications security
Treasurer, controller, chief financial officer
Underwriter

Pathologist
Pharmacist

Private sector executive
Property manager,
Purchasing agent
Recreational therapist
Sales (tangibles)
School administrator
Security guard
Sound technician
Stockbroker
Technical trainer
Transport coordinator

ESTP Career Highlight

Emergency Medical Technicians

EMTs assess the nature of the patient's condition while trying to determine whether the patient has any pre-existing medical conditions. Following medical protocols and guidelines, they provide appropriate emergency care and, when necessary, transport the patient.

Education
High School Diploma and/or 1-2 years formal training

Salary/ Wage

Median Annual Income	$27,070
Median Hourly Income	$13.04

ESTP (Extraverted, Sensing, Thinking, Perceiving) Careers

Actor/performer
Artist
Auditor
Budget analyst

Air traffic controller
Audiovisual specialist
Banker
Car sales

Chef
Civil engineer
Computer programmer
Corrections officer
Dancer
Developer of electronic games
Electrical engineer/electronics specialist
Emergency medical technician (EMT)
Entertainment agent
Exercise physiologist/sports medicine
Financial advisor
Flight engineer/instructor
Franchise owner
Insurance adjuster/agent/broker
Intelligence specialist
Investigator
Laboratory technologist
Landscape architect
Marine biologist
Medical technician
Network integration specialist
Paramedic
Pharmacist
Pilot
Probation officer
Professional athlete
Property manager
Real estate agent
Retail sales
Sports merchandise sales
Stockbroker
Studio, stage, and special effects technician
Surveyor
Teacher (technical, trade)
Television camera operator
Wholesaler

Chiropractor
Coach
Construction/building inspector
Criminalist or ballistics expert
Detective
Eco-tourism specialist

Entrepreneur

Fitness instructor/trainer
Forester
Industrial/mechanical engineer
Insurance fraud investigator
Internet marketer
Investor
Land developer
Management consultant
Marketing personnel
Musician
News reporter
Park naturalist
Photographer
Police officer
Product safety engineer
Promoter
Radio/TV talk show host
Respiratory therapist
Soil conservationist
Sportscaster

Systems support operator/installer
Technical trainer
Tour guide/agent
Wilderness adventure leader

INFJ Career Highlight

Merchandise Designer/Displayer

Creates functional and aesthetic designs that help boost productivity, increase sales, or attract customers Responsible for planning layout of the space and decorating. Develops drawings, presentations, and cost estimates and coordinates the work of contractors.

Education
Bachelor's preferably in Interior Design

Salary/ Wage
Median Annual Income	$37,146
Median Hourly Income	$17.86

INFJ (Introverted, Intuitive, Feeling, Judging) Careers

Adult day care coordinator
Artist
Career counselor
Child welfare counselor
Clergy
Corporate/team trainer
Costume and wardrobe specialist
Customer relations manager
Dietitian/nutritionist
Director, social service agency
Documentary film-maker
Editor/art director (magazines)
Educational program director
Employee assistance program coordinator
Environmental lawyer
Film editor
Fund-raising director
Grant coordinator
Holistic health practitioner
Human resource manager/recruiter
Interior designer

Architect
Bilingual education teacher
Child life specialist
Chiropractor
Coach
Corrective therapist
Crisis hotline operator
Desktop publisher/editor
Director of religious education
Diversity manager,
Editor/art director (Web sites)
Educational consultant
Educational software developer

Exhibit designer
Freelance media planner
Genealogist
Health care administrator
Home economist
Informational-graphics designer
Interpreter/translator

Job analyst	Legal mediator
Legislative assistant	Librarian/informational specialist
Marketer	Massage therapist
Mediator/conflict resolver	Medical doctor
Mental health counselor	Merchandise designer/displayer
Multimedia producer	Museum research worker
Musician	Novelist
Occupational therapist	
Organizational development consultant	
Instructor, child development	Pharmacist
Philanthropic consultant	Photographer
Planned-giving officer	Playwright
Poet	
Preferred customer sales representative	
Psychiatrist	Psychologist
Public health educator	Religious worker
Set designer	Social scientist
Social worker	Special education teacher
Speech-language pathologist/audiologist	
Technology advocate	Substance abuse counselor
Teacher (liberal arts)	Universal design architect

INFP Career Highlight

Human Resources Recruiter

Recruiters maintain contacts within the community and may travel considerably, often to college campuses, to search for promising job applicants. Recruiters screen, interview, and occasionally test applicants. They also may check references and extend job offers.

Education
Bachelor's in Liberal Arts/ Business/ Technical field

Salary/ Wage
Median Annual Income	$42,420
Median Hourly Income	$20.39

INFP (Introverted, Intuitive, Feeling, Perceiving) Careers

Actor

Artist

Biological scientist

Child life specialist

Clinical psychologist

College professor (humanities)

Consultant—team building/conflict resolution

Corporate team trainer

Curator

Desktop publisher

Diversity manager

Editor

Educational software developer

Engagement manager

Ethicist

Film editor

Geneticist

Health technician

Home health social worker

Human resources development specialist

Human resources recruiter

Informational graphics designer

Journalist

Legal mediator

Manual arts therapist

Missionary

Musician

Outplacement consultant

Physical therapist

Psychologist

Public health nurse

Religious worker

Set designer

Social worker

Speech-language pathologist/audiologist

Technology advocate

Writer (poet, novelist)

Architect

Bilingual education teacher

Career counselor

Child welfare counselor

Coach

Composer

Counselor

Customer relations manager

Dietitian/nutritionist

Early childhood education teacher

Educational consultant

Employee assistance counselor

Entertainer

Fashion designer

Genealogist

Grant coordinator

Holistic health practitioner

Industrial organization psychologist

Interior designer

Labor relations specialist

Librarian

Minister/priest

Multimedia producer

Occupational therapist

Philanthropic consultant

Planned-giving officer

Public health educator

Religious educator

Researcher

Social scientist

Special education teacher

Translator/interpreter

INTJ Career Highlight

Electrical/ Electronics Tech

Electrical/Electronics Technician install, adjust, or maintain equipment, including sound, sonar, security, navigation, and surveillance systems on trains, watercraft, or other vehicles. They also inspect, test, maintain, or repair electrical equipment used in factories.

Education
Bachelor's preferably in Interior Design

Salary/ Wage
Median Annual Income $41,433
Median Hourly Income $19.92

INTJ (Introverted, Intuitive, Thinking, Judging) Careers

Academic curriculum designer	Administrator
Aeronautical engineer	Aerospace engineer
Animator	Anthropologist
Architect	Artist
Archivist	Astronomer
Attorney	Auditor
Biologist	Biomedical researcher/engineer
Broadcast engineer	Budget analyst
Business analyst	Cardiologist
Cardiovascular technician	Chemical engineer
City manager	Civil engineer
College professor	Columnist, critic, or commentator
Computer engineer	Computer programmer
Computer security specialist	Computer systems analyst
Coroner	Corrections officer
Credit analyst	Criminologist or ballistics expert
Curator	Database administrator
Dentist	Design engineer
Designer	Desktop publishing specialist
Economist	Editor/art director
Education consultant	Electrical/electronic technician
Engineer	Environmental planner/scientist
Exhibit designer/builder	Financial analyst

Financial planner
Graphic designer
Information services developer
Intelligence specialist
Inventor
Java programmer/analyst
Life scientist
Management consultant
Mathematician
Microbiologist
Musician
Network integration specialist
News analyst/writer
Operations research analyst
Pharmaceutical researcher
Photographer
Physicist
Private sector executive
Psychologist
Social scientist
Software and systems researcher/developer
Strategic planner
Systems administrator
Teacher
Telecommunications security provider
Treasurer or controller
Webmaster

Geneticist
Human resources manager
Intellectual properties attorney
International banker
Investment banker
Judge
Local area network administrator
Manager
Metallurgical engineer
Mortgage broker
Network administrator
Neurologist
Nuclear engineer
Pathologist
Pharmacologist
Physical scientist
Pilot
Psychiatrist
Real estate appraiser

Surgeon
Systems analyst

Web developer
Writer/editor

INTP Career Highlight

Physicists

Physicists explore and identify basic principles and laws governing the motion, energy, structure, and interactions of matter to problems in nuclear energy, electronics, optics, materials, communications, aerospace technology, and medical instrumentation.

Education
Ph.D in Physics

Salary/ Wage
Median Annual Income $94,240
Median Hourly Income $45.31

INTP (Introverted, Intuitive, Thinking, Perceiving) Careers

Anthropologist	Archaeologist
Architect	Artist
Astronomer	Biomedical engineer/researcher
Biophysicist	Business analyst
College administrator	College professor (graduate)
Columnist, critic, commentator	Computer animator
Computer engineer	Computer programmer
Computer security specialist	Computer software designer
Constitutional lawyer	Consultant
Corporate finance attorney	Creative writer
Desktop publishing specialist	Economist
Entertainer/ dancer	Entertainment agent
Entrepreneur	Financial analyst/planner
Forensic researcher	Forestry and park ranger
Geneticist	Historian
Information services developer	Informational-graphics designer
Intellectual property attorney	Intelligence specialist
Internet architect	Interpreter/translator
Inventor	Investigator
Investment banker	Java programmer/analyst
Judge	Lawyer
Legal mediator	Logician
Mathematician	Microbiologist
Music arranger/ orchestrator	Musician
Network administrator	Network integration specialist
Neurologist	Occupational therapist
Pharmaceutical researcher	Pharmacist
Philosopher	Photographer
Physicist	Plastic surgeon
Psychiatrist	Psychologist/psychoanalyst
Research and development specialist	
Respiratory therapist	Scientist (chemistry/biology)
Social scientist	Software designer
Software developer	Strategic planner
Systems analyst/database manager	Technical writer
Venture capitalist	Veterinarian
Web developer	Webmaster

ISFJ Career Highlight

Fish and Game Wardens

Fish and Game Wardens Patrol assigned area to prevent fish and game law violations. Investigate reports of damage to crops or property by wildlife. Compile biological data.

Education
High School Diploma, police academy training

Salary/ Wage
Median Annual Income	$48,942
Median Hourly Income	$23.53

ISFJ (Introverted, Sensing, Feeling, Judging) Careers

Artist
Bank Trust Officer
Biologist
Botanist
Clerical supervisor
Computer support specialist
Corrective therapist
Curator
Dental hygienist/technician
Educational administrator
Fashion merchandiser
Franchise owner, retail
Genealogist
Health care administrator
Historian
Home health aide
Hospice worker
Interior decorator
Librarian/ archivist
Medical equipment salesperson
Medical researcher
Merchandise planner
Museum research worker

Athletic Trainer
Biochemist
Bookkeeper
Child life specialist
Computer operator
Corrections officer
Counselor
Customer service representative
Dietitian/nutritionist
Physician
Fish and game warden
Funeral director
Grant coordinator
Health technician
Home economist
Home health social worker
Hotel/motel manager
Jeweler
Massage therapist
Medical records administrator
Medical technologist
Minister
Musician

Nurse
Optician
Paralegal
Pharmaceutical salesperson
Physical therapist
Police identification and records specialist
Probation officer
Religious worker
Secretary
Speech pathologist
Tax preparer
Teacher (preschool)
Title examiner or abstractor

Occupational therapist
Orthodontist
Personnel administrator
Pharmacist/pharmacy technician
Police detective

Real estate agent/broker
Respiratory therapist
Social worker
Surgical technologist/technician
Teacher (K-12)
Teacher (special education)
Veterinarian

ISFP Career Highlight

Jewelers

Jewelers use a variety of common and specialized hand tools and equipment to design and manufacture new pieces of jewelry; cut, set, and polish gem stones; repair or adjust rings, necklaces, bracelets, earrings, and other jewelry; and appraise jewelry, precious metals, and gems.

Education
High School Diploma, police academy training

Salary/ Wage
Median Annual Income	$29,750
Median Hourly Income	$14.30

ISFP (Introverted, Sensing, Feeling, Perceiving) Careers

Administrator
Archaeologist
Beautician
Botanist
Chef
Coach (high school, college)
Counselor
Dancer
Dietitian/ nutritionist

Air traffic controller
Artist/art therapist
Bookkeeper
Cartoonist or animator
Clerical supervisor
Computer operator
Crisis hotline operator
Dental hygienist/assistant
Exercise physiologist

Fashion designer
Firefighter
Florist
Genealogist
Horticulturist
Insurance fraud investigator
Jeweler
Legal secretary
Marine biologist
Medical technician
Museum curator
Nurse
Optician/ optometrist
Paralegal
Personal fitness trainer
Pharmacist
Physician
Police/corrections officer
Public relations specialist
Recreational therapist
Soil conservationist
Storekeeper
Surgical technologist
Systems analyst
Teacher (preschool)
Television camera operator
Typist
Zoologist

Filmmaker
Fish and game warden
Forester
Geologist
Insurance appraiser/examiner
Interior designer
Landscape architect
Librarian
Media specialist
Merchandise planner
Musician/composer
Occupational therapist
Painter
Pediatrician
Pharmaceutical researcher
Physical therapist
Pilot (commercial)
Psychologist
Recreation worker
Social worker
Speech language pathologist
Surgeon
Surveyor
Teacher (science, art, music)
Teacher (special education)
Translator/interpreter
Veterinarian

ISTJ Career Highlight

Accountants

Accountants and auditors analyze and communicate financial information for various entities such as companies, individual clients, and government. They prepare, analyze, and verify financial documents in order to provide information to clients.

Education
High School Diploma, police academy training
Salary/ Wage
Median Annual Income	$54,630
Median Hourly Income	$26.26

ISTJ (Introverted, Sensing, Thinking, Judging) Careers

Accountant

Architect

Association manager/advisor

Bank examiner

Biomedical technologist

Computer engineer

Construction manager

Corrections officer

Court clerk

Criminalist or ballistics expert

Dentist

Efficiency expert/analyst

Environmental science technician

Exercise physiologist

Fire prevention and protection specialist

Geologist

Hardware engineer

Immigration and customs inspector

Industrial safety and health engineer

Insurance claims examiner/underwriter

Investment securities officer

Judge

Landscape architect

Librarian

Mechanical/industrial/electrical engineer

Medical records technician

Meteorologist

Office manager

Orthodontist

Pharmacist/pharmacy technician

Pilot (commercial)

Probation officer

Public health officer

Purchasing agent and contract specialist

Real estate agent

School principal

Statistician

Surgical technologist

Tax preparer and examiner

Teacher (technical, industrial, math, physical education)

Technical writer

Actuary

Archivist

Auditor

Biology specimen technician

Chief information officer

Computer programmer/specialist

Coroner

Cost estimator

Credit analyst

Database administrator

EEG technologist/technician

Environmental inspector

Estate planner

Government employee

Hardware/software tester

IRS agent

Lab technologist

Law researcher

Manager/supervisor

Medical researcher

Nursing administrator

Optometrist

Paralegal/legal secretary

Physician

Police officer/detective

Property manager

Regulatory compliance officer

Sport equipment/merchandise sales

Surgeon

Systems analyst

Treasurer/controller/chief financial officer
Veterinarian   Web editor
Word processing specialist

If you have not played **Drive of Your Life** game and researched at least 20 careers. Go to it now at

www.escapetocollege.com

Click on the **Follow Your Inner Compass** tab

Write down the career titles you researched here

_____   _____
_____   _____
_____   _____
_____   _____
_____   _____
_____   _____
_____   _____
_____   _____
_____   _____
_____   _____

Do any specific careers get your attention? Write them here.

_____   _____
_____   _____
_____   _____

CHAPTER 9   ELITE GENIUS GROOMING

As you researched many of the careers have you noticed that many of them require some post secondary training? Rather it is a 4 year college, 2 year college, apprenticeship, or certificate it requires some after high school training. But have you ever asked your self, *"Why must I go to school while it is not preparing me for the career I am planning? School seems to be so dull and irrelevant to my future."*

The initial purpose of secondary school was to select the elite who would rule the government. Thomas Jefferson postulated a plan for public education as early as 1778. It called for three distinct grades of education: elementary schools for all children; secondary schools for further common education for the more capable; college and university for the teaching of the sciences in their highest degree and to the most capable.

Each ward would have its common school on the elementary level (1st -4th) for the teaching of reading, writing, and arithmetic. The school would be supported by the ward, and each child would attend three years free of charge and as much longer as the parents wish at their own expense.

These wards would be under the scrutiny of supervisors who would annually select from each ward the most promising children for further education. His plan called for twenty secondary schools (5th grade through 11th) scattered across Virginia where these select students would study Greek, Latin, geography and higher arithmetic. One **"genius"** would be selected from each school every year or two for six more years of advanced study. At the end of the six years the best ten of the twenty would be sent on to a university for three years, the rest dismissed.

He insisted that this plan would provide a basic education for all, rich and poor alike, and that it would make possible advanced training for Virginia's brightest youth, who would otherwise be lost to the state's great need for talent.

In the early history of our country only the elite could become leaders and managers while everyone else was stuck as laborers. Today, a person can decide whether they will become a leader, manager and laborer.

Leadership is one of the world's oldest preoccupations, serving as both a hot topic and an important driver of innovation for thousands of years (Bass, 1990). Effective leadership remains one of the most misunderstood human phenomenon and comprises one of the most fundamental aspects of the human condition (Wren, 1995). Leaders establish direction. Leaders look into the future in anticipation of the organization's or society's global needs and long-term future. Leaders seek to develop new goals and align organizations (Kotter, 1990; Zaleznik, 1998). Leaders motivate and inspire. Leaders produce the potential for dramatic change, chaos, and even failure (Kotter, 1990).

On the other hand, management is a fairly new phenomenon. The emergence of large, complex organizations in the last century generated the need for a system to regulate work and deal with authority and control issues. This resulted in the modern workplace manager who was expected to reduce the internal chaos of those more complicated organizations. Managers control laborers and solve problems. Managers brought order and consistency to the multitude of workplace processes. Since that time, the duties of workplace management and its associated processes have been researched, refined, and improved significantly in the past century (Kotter, 1990, 1995). Managers, however, plan and budget.

Managers have a narrow purpose and try to maintain order, stabilize work, and organize resources continually planning, organizing, supervising, and controlling resources to achieve organizational goals. Planning is associated with providing what the customer wants and developing a way to provide it. Organizing and supervising involves developing an organizational structure, reward systems, and a performance management system. Controlling involves measuring processes and product characteristics, sustaining production processes, reducing variation, providing customer satisfaction, and anticipating short-term needs. Managers take responsibility for those processes and are constantly seeking to improve them.[37]

Laborer is a person who does all the work. There are two times more laborers than managers and leaders combined. They do all the work and often receive a little of the pay.

Managers and leaders attend college and universities albeit for different reasons. Managers attend college to secure a diploma - a credential to prove to the world they have the ability to think and solve problems. They are highly recruited by leaders. Leaders attend college to learn how to innovate, create and develop new profitable products. Make no mistake, leaders and managers make the highest income levels in the world. Laborers earn whatever managers and leaders decided to pay them.

It appears everyone starts out as a laborer and work their way up society's chain. That is true, except managers and leaders are there for a short amount of time. Just enough to determine what problem needs to be solved and what new product needs to be developed. The question, is *"What level of society to you what to be in?"*

Leader? Manager? Laborer?

Execution of your dream will dictate where you land. No execution it is guaranteed you will be a laborer. The problem is as society moves further and further into the Jetson's age there will be fewer and fewer laborers and more and more managers. They will be managing robots but mangers nonetheless. The current recession is proving this management theory to be true. If you desire to be employed to generate the incomes to fuel your dream, you must aim to become a manager or leader.

Public education once only groomed the elite to the university level. Today every person can start life in poverty and rise to great wealth through education, Free of Charge thanks to Alexander Campbell and Horace Mann.

Alexander Campbell in 1841 states the objectives of primary education, which he calls the seven arts. They are

the art of thinking
the art of speaking
the art of reading

the art of singing
the art of writing
the art of calculating
the art of bookkeeping

While these arts have changed as inventions have been created, each of these arts are necessary to survive within the world. He fought rigorously that these arts create a fully functioning productive cultured individual.

As the Industrial Revolution raged on education moved from the selection of one genius per school to creating each child into a genius equalizing every citizen. America needs the mental power of each citizen to continue the growth of our country. Horace Mann, Twelfth Annual Report of Horace Mann as Secretary of Massachusetts State Board of Education.(1848) states *"Education, then, beyond all other devices of human origin, is the great equalizer of the conditions of men -- the balance-wheel of the social machinery. "*

Education began with the philosophy every citizen was intelligent and needed the motivation to expand their intelligence. William Butler Yeats stated *"Education is not the filling of a pail, but the lighting of a fire."* The purpose of school is to make you more intelligent than you were when you began. Its purpose was to light the fire of your genius, to challenge you to prepare you to become a productive cultured citizen

Somewhere around World War II when schools had more children ever in the history of America, education changed into a factorized filing of pails. It was easier to teach lots of children by creating an one size fits all lecture based teaching. While this schooling is dull and boring schools still have the same purpose to create geniuses to light your fire.

High school is the foundation for advanced grooming of geniuses. Those who moved into higher education of college and then university study were prepared for leadership roles in our country. Today that plan is live and well. When students refuse to finish high school and finish college they are basically telling the world I do not desire to be prepared for leadership.

Right now you are thinking, "School is a prison you desire to break out." It is, if you see it a something the government is forcing you to attend. But imagine if you saw it as a place to groom you into the genius you are.

Genius Defined

A **genius** is someone who successfully applies a previously unknown technique in the production of a work of art, science, or calculation, or who masters and personalizes a known technique. A genius possesses great intelligence and remarkable abilities in a specific subject or shows an exceptional natural capacity of intellect and/or ability, especially in the production of creative and original work, something that has never been seen or evaluated previously. Traits often associated with genius include strong individuality, imagination, uniqueness, and innovative drive.

Genius= Creativity + Intelligence

Genius Questionnaire

Answer each question with a yes or no.

1. Do you have the ability to draw or perform musically?
2. Do you have the ability to think differently creating new concepts?
3. Do you have the ability to see both sides of an issue?
4. Do you know that anything is possible?
5. Do you knowing that the experts may be wrong?
6. Do you have the ability to detect and recognize patterns?
7. Do you have the ability to perform mental math in daily life?
8. Do you innovate and create new ways to perform daily tasks?
9. Do you like to create crafts during your free time?
10. Do you daydream or fantasize often?
11. Are you an individual moving in a direction different from the masses?
12. Are you a loner?

Answer YES to 7 or more questions. You are a Genius. Walk into your school with a GENIUS attitude of self discovery, imagination, innovation and self challenge.

Rather than seeing that test as drudgery tell yourself it is another opportunity to prove your genius as you will ACE it. You will earn an A or 100%

Rather than skip the homework, look at it as skill preparation to expand you genius. Complete the homework and turn it in on time. Hint: School is based on homework completion. It makes up a large chunk of a class grade.

Rather than looking at your Grade Point Average (G.P.A.) and report card as rubbish, look at it as a piece of paper to confirm your genius. The higher your Grade Point Average, the more others will see you as the genius you are. Aim to get the highest G.P.A. Hint: Those with the highest G.P.A.s rule the school and have the most fun. If you are a leader ascend to your throne. Get that high G.P.A.

Rather than looking at that research project or essay as another unnecessary activity look at as an opportunity to discover your new situations, likes and dislikes, your interests. Maya Angelou states *"Education helps one cease being intimidated by strange situations."* "What holds some of our young people back is a feeling of intimidation - the sense that they do not have the stuff inside to enter the game and compete. Education affords our children a knowledge of themselves and a recognition of their strength and abilities. Education allows our children to discover they can adapt to new situations and thrive." as quoted in *Eric Copage's book,* ***Black Pearls for Parents.***

Here is a list of items you could learn while at school. Which one of these interest do you like? Check the like circle. Can you incorporate any of these interest into one of your current classes?

For Example   **Direct a play.**

You could ask you English teacher if you could write a screenplay in place of an essay assignment. Once the screenplay has been grade, you will direct and produce the play you wrote.

O'Net Interest Profiler

No.		Like	Unsure	Dislike
1.	Build kitchen cabinets	☐	☐	☐
2.	Guard money in an armored car	☐	☐	☐
3.	Study space travel	☐	☐	☐
4.	Make a map of the bottom of an ocean	☐	☐	☐
5.	Conduct a symphony orchestra	☐	☐	☐
6.	Write stories or articles for magazines	☐	☐	☐
7.	Teach an individual an exercise routine	☐	☐	☐
8.	Performing nursing duties in a hospital	☐	☐	☐
9.	Buy and sell stocks and bonds	☐	☐	☐
10.	Manage a retail store	☐	☐	☐
11.	Develop a spreadsheet using computer software	☐	☐	☐
12.	Proofread records or forms	☐	☐	☐
13.	Operate a dairy farm	☐	☐	☐
14.	Lay brick or tile	☐	☐	☐
15.	Study the history of past civilizations	☐	☐	☐
16.	Study animal behavior	☐	☐	☐
17.	Direct a play	☐	☐	☐
18.	Create dance routines for a show	☐	☐	☐
19.	Give CPR to someone who has stopped breathing	☐	☐	☐
20.	Help people with personal or emotional problems	☐	☐	☐

21.	Sell telephone and other communication equipment	☐	☐	☐
22.	Operate a beauty salon or barber shop	☐	☐	☐
23.	Use a computer program to generate customer bills	☐	☐	☐
24.	Schedule conferences for an organization	☐	☐	☐
25.	Monitor a machine on an assembly line	☐	☐	☐
26.	Repair household appliances	☐	☐	☐
27.	Develop a new machine	☐	☐	☐
28.	Plan a research study	☐	☐	☐
29.	Write books or plays	☐	☐	☐
30.	Play a musical instrument	☐	☐	☐
31.	Teach children how to read	☐	☐	☐
32.	Work with mentally disabled children	☐	☐	☐
33.	Sell merchandise over the telephone	☐	☐	☐
34.	Run a stand that sells newspapers and magazines	☐	☐	☐
35.	Keep accounts payable/receivable for an office	☐	☐	☐
36.	Load computer software into a large computer network	☐	☐	☐
37.	Drive a taxi cab	☐	☐	☐
38.	Install flooring in houses	☐	☐	☐
39.	Study ways to reduce water pollution	☐	☐	☐
40.	Develop a new medical treatment or procedure	☐	☐	☐
41.	Perform comedy routines in front of an audience	☐	☐	☐
42.	Perform as an extra in movies, plays or television shows	☐	☐	☐

No.		Like	Unsure	Dislike
43.	Teach an elementary school class	☐	☐	☐
44.	Give career guidance to people	☐	☐	☐
45.	Give a presentation about a product you are selling	☐	☐	☐

No.		Like	Unsure	Dislike
46.	Buy and sell land	☐	☐	☐
47.	Transfer funds between banks using a computer	☐	☐	☐
48.	Organize and schedule office meetings	☐	☐	☐
49.	Raise fish in a fish hatchery	☐	☐	☐
50.	Build a brick walkway	☐	☐	☐
51.	Determine the infection rate of a new disease	☐	☐	☐
52.	Study rocks and minerals	☐	☐	☐
53.	Write reviews of books or plays	☐	☐	☐
54.	Compose or arrange music	☐	☐	☐
55.	Supervise the activities of children at a camp	☐	☐	☐
56.	Help people with family-related problems	☐	☐	☐
57.	Sell compact disks and tapes at a music store	☐	☐	☐
58.	Run a toy store	☐	☐	☐
59.	Use a word processor to edit and format documents	☐	☐	☐
60.	Operate a calculator	☐	☐	☐
61.	Assemble electronic parts	☐	☐	☐
62.	Drive a truck to deliver packages to offices and homes	☐	☐	☐
63.	Diagnose and treat sick animals	☐	☐	☐

64.	Study the personalities of world leaders	☐	☐	☐
65.	Act in a movie	☐	☐	☐
66.	Dance in a Broadway show	☐	☐	☐
67.	Perform rehabilitation therapy	☐	☐	☐
68.	Do volunteer work at a non-profit organization	☐	☐	☐
69.	Manage the operations of a hotel	☐	☐	☐
70.	Sell houses	☐	☐	☐
71.	Direct or transfer phone calls for a large organization	☐	☐	☐
72.	Perform office filing tasks	☐	☐	☐
73.	Paint houses	☐	☐	☐
74.	Enforce fish and game laws	☐	☐	☐
75.	Conduct chemical experiments	☐	☐	☐
76.	Conduct biological research	☐	☐	☐
77.	Draw pictures	☐	☐	☐
78.	Sing professionally	☐	☐	☐
79.	Help elderly people with their daily activities	☐	☐	☐
80.	Teach children how to play sports	☐	☐	☐
81.	Sell candy and popcorn at sports events	☐	☐	☐
82.	Manage a supermarket	☐	☐	☐
83.	Compute and record statistical and other numerical data	☐	☐	☐
84.	Generate the monthly payroll checks for an office	☐	☐	☐
85.	Operate a grinding machine in a factory	☐	☐	☐
86.	Work on an offshore oil-drilling rig	☐	☐	☐

87.	Study the population growth of a city	☐	☐	☐
88.	Study whales and other types of marine life	☐	☐	☐
89.	Perform stunts for a movie or television show	☐	☐	☐
90.	Create special effects for movies	☐	☐	☐

No.		Like	Unsure	Dislike
91.	Help disabled people improve their daily living skills	☐	☐	☐
92.	Teach sign language to people with hearing disabilities	☐	☐	☐
93.	Manage a department within a large company	☐	☐	☐
94.	Sell a soft drink product line to stores and restaurants	☐	☐	☐
95.	Take notes during a meeting	☐	☐	☐
96.	Keep shipping and receiving records	☐	☐	☐
97.	Perform lawn care services	☐	☐	☐
98.	Assemble products in a factory	☐	☐	☐
99.	Investigate crimes	☐	☐	☐
100.	Study the movement of planets	☐	☐	☐
101.	Conduct a musical choir	☐	☐	☐
102.	Act in a play	☐	☐	☐
103.	Help people who have problems with drugs or alcohol	☐	☐	☐
104.	Help conduct a group therapy session	☐	☐	☐
105.	Sell refreshments at a movie theater	☐	☐	☐
106.	Sell hair-care products to stores and salons	☐	☐	☐
107.	Calculate the wages of employees	☐	☐	☐

108.	Assist senior-level accountants in performing bookkeeping tasks	☐	☐	☐
109.	Catch fish as a member of a fishing crew	☐	☐	☐
110.	Refinish furniture	☐	☐	☐
111.	Examine blood samples using a microscope	☐	☐	☐
112.	Investigate the cause of a fire	☐	☐	☐
113.	Paint sets for plays	☐	☐	☐
114.	Audition singers and musicians for a musical show	☐	☐	☐
115.	Help families care for ill relatives	☐	☐	☐
116.	Provide massage therapy to people	☐	☐	☐
117.	Start your own business	☐	☐	☐
118.	Negotiate business contracts	☐	☐	☐
119.	Type labels for envelopes and packages	☐	☐	☐
120.	Inventory supplies using a hand-held computer	☐	☐	☐
121.	Fix a broken faucet	☐	☐	☐
122.	Do cleaning or maintenance work	☐	☐	☐
123.	Study the structure of the human body	☐	☐	☐
124.	Develop psychological profiles of criminals	☐	☐	☐
125.	Design sets for plays	☐	☐	☐
126.	Announce a radio show	☐	☐	☐
127.	Plan exercises for disabled patients	☐	☐	☐
128.	Counsel people who have a life-threatening illness	☐	☐	☐
129.	Represent a client in a lawsuit	☐	☐	☐

130.	Negotiate contracts for professional athletes	☐	☐	☐
131.	Develop an office filing system	☐	☐	☐
132.	Keep records of financial transactions for an organization	☐	☐	☐
133.	Maintain the grounds of a park	☐	☐	☐
134.	Operate a machine on a production line	☐	☐	☐
135.	Develop a way to better predict the weather	☐	☐	☐

Hint: Many of your teachers entered education as they have a child-like fun streak. Ignite their fire with your genius ideas. **ASK** until someone says yes.

School is the foundation by which you compete for jobs, college spots, apprenticeship spots, and scholarships. **WHAT YOU PUT INTO YOUR SCHOOL WORK WILL BE REFLECTED AT THE GRADUATION.**

CHAPTER 10   CREDENTIALS - TICKET TO LIFE

College is the grooming place for leader and managers, individuals who have an uncommon sense of the world. How do colleges judge whether students are qualified for their grooming? They set admissions requirements of grade point averages and scores of standardized exams such as ACT or SAT.

Most people think Grade Point Averages (G.P.A.) indicates a person is smart when it highlight the student's ability to complete a task but more importantly the ability to assimilate to an established system. (*Assimilate means to make similar or absorb into the system. When you encounter a word you do not know the definition get in to the habit of consulting a dictionary*) Or for those who need common language they do what the teacher expect them to do. Those who assimilate the most, often achieve more assistance and hence higher grades. Any student can achieve a high G.P.A. if they focus and complete all their homework and class work.

Next students must conquer the ACT or SAT test. Not familiar with the ACT or SAT test. The ACT is a standardized test for high school achievement and college admissions in the United States produced by ACT, Inc. It was first administered in fall 1959 by Everett Franklin Lindquist as a competitor to the College Board's Scholastic Aptitude Test, now the SAT Reasoning Test. Some students who perform poorly on the SAT find that they perform better on the ACT and vice versa. The ACT test has historically consisted of four tests: English, Math, Reading, and Science reasoning. In February 2005, an optional writing test was added to the ACT, mirroring changes to the SAT that took place later in March of the same year. All four-year colleges and universities in the U.S. accept the ACT. The maximum score is 36. The average score by students sitting for the exam is 21.

ACT Score Comparison

If you're wondering if you have the ACT scores you'll need to get into one of these universities in the United States, here's a side-by-side comparison of scores for the middle 50% of enrolled students. If your scores fall within or above these ranges, you're on target for admission to one of these top colleges.

Top University ACT Score Comparison (mid 50%)

	ACT Scores by Percentile					
	Composite		English		Math	
	25%	75%	25%	75%	25%	75%
Carnegie Mellon	29	33	28	34	28	34
Duke	29	34	30	34	29	35
Emory	29	33	-	-	-	-
Georgetown	28	32	28	34	27	33
Johns Hopkins	29	33	24	31	28	34
Northwestern	30	34	30	35	29	34
Stanford	30	34	30	34	29	35
University of Chicago	28	33	29	35	28	34
Vanderbilt	30	33	31	34	29	34
Washington University	31	34	32	35	31	35
2007-08 data from National Center for Educational Statistics						

Ivy League ACT Score Comparison (mid 50%)

	ACT Scores by Percentile					
	Composite		English		Math	
	25%	75%	25%	75%	25%	75%
Brown	28	33	28	34	27	34
Columbia	28	33	28	34	27	34
Cornell	28	32	28	34	27	33
Dartmouth	28	34	-	-	-	-

Harvard	31	35	32	35	30	35
Princeton	30	34	30	35	30	35
U Penn	29	33	29	34	28	34
Yale	29	34	-	-	-	-

2007-08 data from National Center for Educational Statistics

Top Public University ACT Scores (mid 50%)

	ACT Scores by Percentile					
	Composite		English		Math	
	25%	75%	25%	75%	25%	75%
College of William and Mary	27	32	27	33	26	30
Georgia Tech	27	31	25	31	27	32
UC Berkeley	23	30	23	31	25	32
UCLA	24	30	24	31	25	31
UC San Diego	23	29	22	29	25	30
University of Illinois at Urbana Champaign	26	31	25	32	26	32
University of Michigan	27	31	26	32	27	32
UNC Chapel Hill	25	30	24	31	25	30
University of Wisconsin	26	30	25	31	26	31

2007-08 data from National Center for Educational Statistics

Your ACT scores can be an important part of your public university application. This article presents a side-by-side comparison of ACT scores for the country's top public universities. If your scores fall within or above these ranges, you're on target for admission to one of these public universities.

ACT scores, of course, are just one part of the application. It's possible to have scores above the averages presented here and still get rejected if other parts of your application are weak. Similarly, some students with scores significantly below the ranges listed here gain admission because they demonstrate other strengths.

Also, if you are an out-of-state applicant, you may need to have scores significantly higher than those shown here. Most public universities give preference to in-state applicants.

Some scholarship and loan agencies may use ACT test results with other information such as high school grades to identify qualified candidates. However, the agencies may not look at academic potential alone. The ACT score report provides information about a student's educational needs, extracurricular achievements, and educational plans. This information, along with high school grades and test scores, helps the agencies evaluate applications for scholarships, loans, and other financial assistance.

The SAT Reasoning Test *(formerly Scholastic Aptitude Test and Scholastic Assessment Test)* is a standardized test for college admissions in the United States. The SAT is owned, published, and developed by the College Board, a non-profit organization in the United States, and was once developed, published, and scored by the Educational Testing Service (ETS). ETS now administers the exam. The College Board claims that the SAT can determine whether or not a person is ready for college. The current SAT Reasoning Test takes three hours and forty-five minutes and costs $45 ($71 International), excluding late fees. Since the SAT's introduction in 1901, its name and scoring has changed several times. In 2005, the test was renamed to the "SAT Reasoning Test" with possible scores from 600 to 2400 combining test results from three 800-point sections *(math, critical reading, and writing)*, along with other subsections scored separately.[38]

Discovered at least three careers that generate a burning passion? Write those careers here.

1. _____

2. _____

3. _____

Each career has educational requirements that are necessary to secure a job in that career. Review your careers and your research and determine specific education you need to enter career. Write them here.

Example: Career interest - **Actuary**
              Education requirement- **Bachelors in Statistics**

1. _____

2. _____

3. _____

Go to **www.escapetocollege.com**. Click on **Follow Your Inner Compass** tab. Go to **Dream Explorer** tab. Login in. Go to **DECIDE** tab. Scroll down to **Program to College** tab. Select a major program you are pursuing in college. Review list of colleges with your program. Research colleges.

Decide if you would fit best at a ----

Small college/trade school
Medium Size College
Large University

In a setting------
              Urban
              Suburban
              Rural

Are you a visual person and need some assistance in making that decision? Visit college campuses online:

Campus Tours	http://www.campustours.com
eCampustour.com	http://www.ecampustours.com/
College ClickTV	http://collegeclicktv.com
YOUniversity TV	http://www.youniversitytv.com

These sites showcase virtual tours of college campuses. Review the tours to decide if you would desire to visit the school. View the schools before you choose to physically visit them.

Desire to visit colleges physically consider the Historical Black Colleges (HBCU) Tour or Hispanic-Serving Institutions (HSIs) tour. Check with your local community organization such as the NAACP or LULAC.

Select 7 colleges you would attend.
List them here.

1. _____

2. _____

3. _____

4. _____

5. _____

6. _____

7. _____

Now let's detail your research for each college now. List pertinent information about them here. If the information is not readily available on the colleges' website call the admissions office and request the information.

School #1 _____

Location _____

Major City _____ **Miles to Major City** _____

Admission G.P.A. _____

Required Admission Exam _____ **Minimum Score** _____

Annual Tuition Room/ Board _____

Maximum Parent Income _____
For 100% tuition package

Admission Rep. _____

Phone _____

School #2 _____

Location _____

Major City _____ **Miles to Major City** _____

Admission G.P.A. _____

Required Admission Exam _____ **Minimum Score** _____

Annual Tuition Room/ Board _____

Maximum Parent Income _____
For 100% tuition package

Admission Rep. _____

Phone _____

School #3 _____

Location _____

Major City _____ **Miles to Major City** _____

Admission G.P.A. _____

Required Admission Exam _____ **Minimum Score** _____

Annual Tuition Room/ Board _____

Maximum Parent Income _____
For 100% tuition package

Admission Rep. _____

Phone _____

School #4 _____

Location _____

Major City _____ **Miles to Major City** _____

Admission G.P.A. _____

Required Admission Exam _____ **Minimum Score** _____

Annual Tuition Room/ Board _____

Maximum Parent Income _____
For 100% tuition package

Admission Rep. _____

Phone _____

School #5 _____

Location _____

Major City _____ **Miles to Major City** _____

Admission G.P.A. _____

Required Admission Exam _____ **Minimum Score** _____

Annual Tuition Room/ Board _____

Maximum Parent Income
For 100% tuition package _____

Admission Rep. _____

Phone _____

School #6 _____

Location _____

Major City _____ **Miles to Major City** _____

Admission G.P.A. _____

Required Admission Exam _____ **Minimum Score** _____

Annual Tuition Room/ Board _____

Maximum Parent Income
For 100% tuition package _____

Admission Rep. _____

Phone _____

School #7 _____

Location _____

Major City _____ **Miles to Major City** _____

Admission G.P.A._____

Required Admission Exam_____ **Minimum Score** _____

Annual Tuition Room/ Board _____

Maximum Parent Income _____
For 100% tuition package

Admission Rep. _____

Phone _____

Knowledge of what a college requires for admission is important to develop your Road Map. It tells you what credentials you must have to be admitted to the higher education institution of your choice.

CHAPTER 11   ESCAPE ROUTE

I was once riding to my family's hometown, Vidalia, GA, where everyone is your cousin. The trip from Detroit is 12 hours straight down I-75. I fell asleep and when I woke up, we were in West Virginia. My cousin stopped to get some gas and got on the wrong highway going southeast rather straight south. I was furious as the trip to me was intuitively simple, 12 hours straight down I-75. It took us 20 hours to get Vidalia. However, I learned a great lesson, *"Many people need to map out a route to remind them where they are going."* In this case an escape route. That lesson applies to adults and students equally.

It is easy to forget why one comes to school. Friends are fun to be around and before we know it we have missed one class and then another, socializing. Those missed classes turn into failed classes, behavior issues, a missed graduation;   at 23 years of age, we are forced to study for the General Equivalency Diploma (GED) as we are now labeled a dropout.

The intent of Escape to College is to develop your unique personal escape route. At this point you should have:

1. Discovered what ancient civilization you descended from
2. Created crazy Outrageous Experiences
3. Created your Future Lifestyle Map
4. Established 101 goals and timeline for those goals
5. Determined passionate interest

6. Selected your career goal
7. Reviewed credentials set plan for improvement
8. Selected 7 college you desire to attend
9. Researched and toured selected colleges

If you have not completed these tasks please go back and do so now. Once these are complete you will compile them into your Educational Development Plan (EDP).

Go to www.escapetocollege.com Click on **Follow Your Inner Compass**. Click the **Dream Explorer** link. Go to the **Plan** tab. Scroll down to the **EDP** tab. Begin to enter **My info**. Enter every category especially the **My Progress** section.

Write the areas you will attempt to improve. Assess the areas of your life you need to improve to achieve your career goal. If your school requires a minimum G.P.A. and you have a 2.5, you need a higher G.P.A., which means you need to either complete and turn in your homework on- time or study more often to achieve higher scores on class test. Either way, you need to act upon your goal.

Suppose, you chose a college that requires an ACT score of 25 or a total SAT score of 1700 including the writing section, You complete the ACT practice test and score a 14, which is 9 points below the required goal. What do you do? You first review the questions you scored wrong and create a study plan to educate yourself on the concepts you do not understand, including your vocabulary as both of the ACT and SAT exams are heavily vocabulary based.

There are other steps you need to complete in your junior year of high school.

10. Registered for standardized exams – ACT and SAT
11. Write your personal statement
12. Research scholarships www.escapetocollege.com
      There are 200+ scholarships
13. Apply for colleges

With good grades and a high G.P.A., colleges will provide you the tuition assistance you need. They will hunt you down. I know this first hand as I attended the University of Michigan on a full ride scholarship after scoring in the 80th percentile on the ACT. I received a Bachelor's of Arts in Economics. That's a great opportunity for a teenager from a Housing Project in Flint, Michigan. I escaped to college, so can you.

NOTE PAGE

NOTE PAGE

INDEX

ESCAPE TO COLLEGE SCHOLARSHIP

Most scholarships present awards to the students with the highest grade point average. Many of the brightest students do not earn the highest grades as they are individuals who "think out of the box" – the entrepreneur. We believe those talented individuals are overlooked and need an incentive to join the academic game of high grade point average and test scores.

Are you going to be a leader or a follower?

5 scholarships of $1000 in 2010

Scholarship requirements
1. Current Spring 2010 7th to 11th Graders
2. Cumulative Grade Point Average 2.0 - 3.0
3. Review **Escape to College** Book cover.
   Determine   name
                         location
                         admissions requirements
                         specialty of college/university

4. One paragraph (5 sentences minimum) detail specific career goal and plan to improve Grade Point Average over the next year.
5. 7th through 11th Preferred College
6. Scholarship entry period is April 1 - June 1, 2010

Apply here. www.upliftinc.org/Escape_to_College.html

This scholarship is managed by Uplift, Inc., a 501 (c) 3 nonprofit Idea Incubator and teen advocacy firm.

Uplift, Inc. can accept donations to this scholarship fund or customize a donor specific fund to assist students in their Escape to College. Call **877-429-2370** or send an email to ida@upliftinc.org to discuss.

NEED A SPEAKER?

During this economic recession, **Ida Byrd-Hill** has an uplifting message of success for your audience, as well as an engaging style that will make your entire organization shift into high-gear, both personally and professionally!

For more than 20 years, Ida Byrd-Hill has studied the elements of what makes successful people successful. She knows what **motivates them, what drives them, and what inspires them**... and she brings this critical insight to your organization.

She can customize a session for your organization based on previous sessions completed. Previous sessions:

LIFESTYLE

A Champagne Toast	Breakin' Out of Your Financial Funk!
Escape to......	Escape to College
Follow Your Inner Compass Teen	Follow Your Inner Compass to Reinvention
Future Lifestyle Map	School Improvement
Transforming from Low to High Performance	What's Your Personality?

FINANCIAL/ BUSINESS

Change Management -	Developing a Goal Setting Culture
Creativity and Innovation – Busting Out	Visualization-Key to Business Growth in Down Economy

If your school, social group, religious organization or company can benefit from the uplifting messages of **Ida Byrd-Hill** and her colleagues,

CONTACT her at info@upheavalmedia.net

or

877-429-2370 to schedule your meeting.

SHARE YOUR SUCCESS STORIES

Did you enjoy **ESCAPE TO COLLEGE**? Tell us your stories. Did you learn more about your family, or yourself? If so, please provide us with your stories.

Please send them by electronic mail to:

info@upheavalmedia.net

Or to

Upheaval Media, Inc.
P.O. Box 241488
Detroit, MI 48224

Please note all stories, pictures etc. become the property of Upheaval Media, Inc. and will not be returned unless sent with a self addressed stamped envelope.

A special gift will be sent to those who provide a physical mailing address.

More Books Written by Ida Byrd-Hill

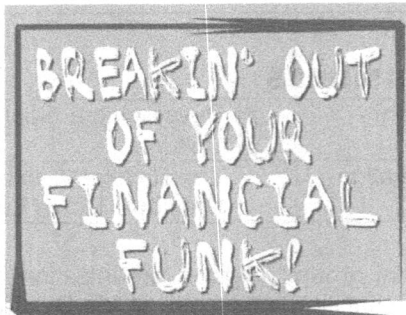

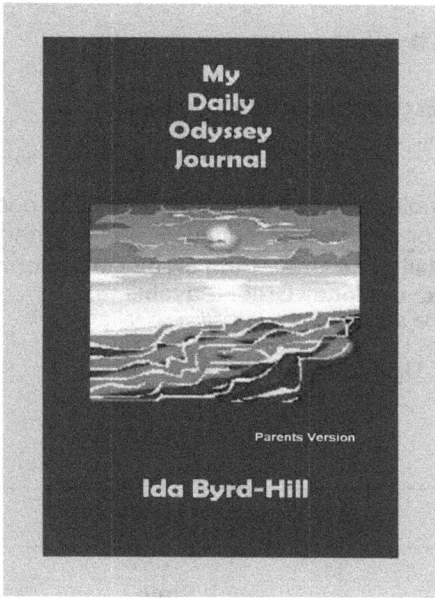

My
Daily
Odyssey
Journal

Parents Version

Ida Byrd-Hill

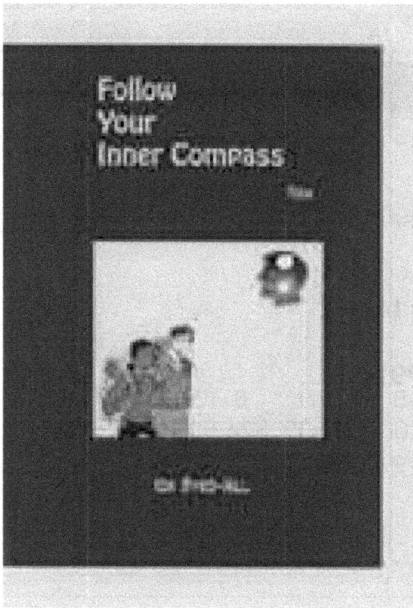

Follow
Your
Inner Compass

BOOK ORDER FORM

Share **Escape to College** with others

Order online at www.upheavalmedia.net

Discounts are available for orders larger than 250 books,
call 877-429-2370 or send email to: info@upheavalmedia.net

Prefer to order by Mail Send Order form credit card information, Check, or Money Order Payable to:

Book will not be shipped until transactions clear the bank.

Upheaval Media, Inc.
P.O. Box 241488
Detroit, MI 48224

Name _____

Address_____

City _____   State _____

Zip _____   Phone _____

Email _____

Credit cards only

Visa   #_____-_____-_____-_____
Mastercard   3 digit Security Code _____
Discover   Name on Card
American Express   _____

Quantity of Books
_____ x $16.98 per book   =   _____

Shipping & Handling

1	2-3	4-5	6-7	8-10
$4.50	$10.50	$15.00	$20.00	$24.00

Shipping & Handling Total   =   _____

Total Amount   =   _____
Book Title _____

BIBLIOGRAPHY

1 www.wikipedia

2 http://www.terrafugia.com/

3 Boyle, Alan, Space hotel by 2010? MSNBC September 22, 2006

4 Genesis II completes 10,000 Orbits!- Nevada Acquisition April 23, 2009

5 Hadhazy, Adam, Forget the Dark Knight--the White Knight Two mothership has arrived Scientific American July 28, 2008

6 ABC news

7 Onishi, Norimitsu, In a Wired South Korea, Robots Will Feel Right at Home, New York Times Asia Pacific April 2, 2006

8 Wiki iPhone

9 Antone Gonsalves, Sales of Nintendo Wii Play Surpass 10 Million Mark InformationWeek, March 20, 2009

10 2008 Sales, Demographics and Usage Data Essential Facts About The Computer and Video Game Industry, Entertainment Software Association

11 Clive Thompson The Netbook Effect: How Cheap Little Laptops Hit the Big Time, WIRED magazine, 02.23.09

12 Florida, Richard, The Rise of the Creative Class. and how it's transforming work leisure, community and every day life, Basic Books New York, NY 2002

13 Bureau of Labor Statistics

14 Gartner, February 2008

15 The Partnership for 21st Century is a partnership of education and corporate leaders who collaborate on how to prepare students for the workforce they need today and tomorrow.

16 Onishi, Norimitsu, In a Wired South Korea, Robots Will Feel Right at Home, New York Times Asia Pacific April 2, 2006

17 http://www.edu.cn/20010101/21803.shtml

18 The Malaysian Smart School A Conceptual Blueprint 1997 http://www.msc.com.my/smartschool/downloads/blueprint.pdf

19 PISA 2006 Science Competencies for Tomorrow's World

20 Assessing Scientific, Reading and Mathematical Literacy: A Framework for PISA 2006

21 Gamerman, Ellen, What Makes Finnish Kids So Smart? Finland's teens score extraordinarily high on an international test. American educators are trying to figure out why. Wall Street Journal Helsinki, Finland February 29, 2008

22 Gamerman, Ellen, What Makes Finnish Kids So Smart? Finland's teens score extraordinarily high on an international test. American educators are trying to figure out why. Wall Street Journal Helsinki, Finland February 29, 2008

23 Gamerman, Ellen, What Makes Finnish Kids So Smart? Finland's teens score extraordinarily high on an international test. American educators are trying to figure out why. Wall Street Journal Helsinki, Finland February 29, 2008

24 Nash, Madeline, "How A Child's Brain Develops." TIME Magazine, February 3, 1997

25 Montessori, Maria, The Secret of Childhood, Fides Publisher 1966

26 Allen, James. As a Man Thinketh, 1902

27 The Bible

28 Dictionary.com

29 Byrd-Hill, Ida. Breakin' Out of Your Financial Funk, Upheaval Media, 2008

30Hewitt, Andrew and d'Abadie ,Luc. The Power of Focus for College Students, HCI Books, 2005

31 Hewitt, Andrew and d'Abadie ,Luc. The Power of Focus for College Students, HCI Books, 2005

32 Baron, Renee. What Type am I? Discover who you really are? Penguin Books, 1998

33 www.famoustypes.com

34 Kroeger. Otto. Type Talk The 16 Personality types that determine how we live, love and work, Delta 1988

35 www.careervoyages.gov Top 50 Demand Occupations 2009

36 Ball State career resources center

37 Kotterman, Leaders vs Management The Quality of Management Journal Summer 2006

38 www.wikipedia.com

www.ingramcontent.com/pod-product-compliance
Lightning Source LLC
Chambersburg PA
CBHW071222290326
41931CB00037B/1850

* 9 7 8 0 6 1 5 3 6 2 6 6 3 *